Gottlieb Mittelberger, Carl Theodor Eben

Gottlieb Mittelberger's journey to Pennsylvania in the year 1750 and return to Germany in the year 1754

Gottlieb Mittelberger, Carl Theodor Eben

Gottlieb Mittelberger's journey to Pennsylvania in the year 1750 and return to Germany in the year 1754

ISBN/EAN: 9783744745758

Printed in Europe, USA, Canada, Australia, Japan

Cover: Foto ©Andreas Hilbeck / pixelio.de

More available books at **www.hansebooks.com**

Gottlieb Mittelbergers
Reise
nach
Pennsylvanien
im Jahr 1750.
und
Rükreise nach Teutschland
im Jahr 1754.
Enthaltend
nicht nur eine Beschreibung des Landes
nach seinem gegenwärtigen Zustande, son-
dern auch eine ausführliche Nachricht von den
unglükseligen und betrübten Umständen der meisten
Teutschen, die in dieses Land gezogen sind,
und dahin ziehen.

Stuttgard,
gedrukt bey Gottlub Friderich Jenisch. 1756.

GOTTLIEB MITTELBERGER'S

JOURNEY

TO

PENNSYLVANIA

IN THE YEAR 1750

AND

RETURN TO GERMANY

IN THE YEAR 1754.

CONTAINING

NOT ONLY A DESCRIPTION OF THE COUNTRY ACCORDING TO
ITS PRESENT CONDITION, BUT ALSO A DETAILED ACCOUNT
OF THE SAD AND UNFORTUNATE CIRCUMSTANCES OF
MOST OF THE GERMANS THAT HAVE EMIGRATED,
OR ARE EMIGRATING TO THAT COUNTRY.

TRANSLATED FROM THE GERMAN

BY

CARL THEO. EBEN,

MEMBER OF THE GERMAN SOCIETY OF PENNSYLVANIA.

PHILADELPHIA
JOHN JOS. McVEY.
1898.

IN rendering G. Mittelberger's *Reise nach Pennsylvanien* into English, it has been the translator's aim to reproduce the author's work with the greatest possible accuracy consistent with grammatical correctness, photographing, as it were, the quaint and naïve language of the original, although at the sacrifice of elegant diction. In a few instances, where it seemed necessary to make the author's meaning clear, a word or brief remark has been added to the text in brackets [ ], or a note at the foot of the page.

TO THE

MOST ILLUSTRIOUS PRINCE AND

LORD,

CARL,

DUKE OF WÜRTEMBERG AND TECK, COUNT OF MÖMPELGARDT, LORD OF HEIDENHEIM AND JUSTINGEN, ETC., KNIGHT OF THE GOLDEN FLEECE, AND FIELD-MAR-SHAL-GENERAL OF THE LAUD-ABLE SWABIAN CIRCLE, ETC.

TO MY MOST GRACIOUS PRINCE

AND LORD

DEDICATES IN DEEPEST SUBMISSION

IN ITS NOW IMPROVED FORM

THE PRESENT HUMBLE PUBLICATION

WHICH

YOUR ILLUSTRIOUS PRINCELY HIGHNESS

HAS GRACIOUSLY DEIGNED TO PERUSE

PARTLY

IN MANUSCRIPT,

AND

COMMENDS HIMSELF TO A CONTINUANCE

OF YOUR HIGH

PRINCELY GRACE AND FAVOR.

GOTTLIEB MITTELBERGER.

The communications from the realm of nature, the animals, plants, etc., will no less arrest the attention of the reader, inasmuch as the wise Creator has placed an entirely new theatre of his miracles before the eyes of rational man. But the most important part of this publication will no doubt be found in the account of the fate that awaits most of the unfortunate people who leave Germany to seek uncertain prospects in the New World, but find instead, if not death, most surely an oppressive servitude and slavery. Nothing has been changed in the author's work, except that some notes from other writers of repute, confirming the author's narrative, have been added on the margin, and that the orthography has been made to conform to that in general use. The little work is herewith warmly recommended to the reader.

JOURNEY

JOURNEY TO PENNSYLVANIA IN AMERICA.

IN the month of May, 1750, I departed from Enzweihingen, Vaihingen County, my native place, for Heilbronn, where an organ stood ready to be shipped and sent to Pennsylvania. With this organ, I sailed the usual way, down the Neckar and Rhine to Rotterdam in Holland. From Rotterdam I sailed with a transport of about 400 souls, Würtembergers, Durlachers, Palatines and Swiss, etc., across the North Sea to Kaupp [Cowes] in England, and after a sojourn of 9 days there, across the great ocean, until I landed in Philadelphia, the capital of Pennsylvania, Oct. 10, 1750.* From home to Rotterdam, including my sojourn there, I spent 7 weeks, caused by the many stoppages down the Rhine and in Holland, whereas this journey could otherwise

---

* In the list of names of Foreigners arriving in the ship "Osgood," William Wilkie, Captain, from Rotterdam, and taking the oath of allegiance Sept. 29th, 1750 [O. S.], is that of Gottlieb Mittelberger.—Penna. Archives, 2nd Series, Vol. XVII., p. 324.

be made swifter; but from Rotterdam to Philadelphia the voyage lasted 15 weeks. I was nearly 4 years in that country, engaged, as my testimonials show, as organist and schoolmaster with the German St. Augustine's Church in Providence, having besides given private instruction in music and in the German language, as the following certificate will show, at the house of Captain Diemer.

Whereas the Bearer, Mr. Mittelberger, Music Master, has resolved to return from this Province, to his native Land, which is in the Dukedom of Würtemberg in High Germany; I have at his Request granted these Lines to certify that ye above nam'd Mr. Mittelberger has behaved himself honestly, diligently, and faithfully in ye Offices of Schoolmaster and Organist, during ye Space of three Years; in ye Township of New-Providence, County of Philadelphia and Province of Pennsylvania, etc. So that I and all his Employers were entirely satisfied, and would willingly have him to remain with us. But as his Call obliges him to proceed on his long Journey; we would recommend ye s'd Mr. Mittelberger to all Persons of Dignity and Character; and beg their Assistance, so that he may pass and repass untill he arrives at his Respective Abode; which may God grant, and

and may ye Benediction of Heaven accompany him in his Journey. Deus benedicat susceptis ejus & ferat eum ad amicos suos maxima prosperitate.

Dabam, Providentiæ Philadelphiæ
  Comitatu Pennsylvania in America, die 25. Apr. A. D. 1754.

                  John Diemer, Cap.
                  Sam. Kennedy, M. D.
                  Henery Pawling, Esqr.

    T.
Henry Marsteller.
Matthias Gmelin.

I have carefully inquired into the condition of the country; and what I describe here, I have partly experienced myself, and partly heard from trustworthy people who were familiar with the circumstances. I might possibly be able to relate a great deal more, if I had thought that I should ever publish something about Pennsylvania. For I always considered myself far too weak for such an undertaking. But the fatalities which I suffered on my journey to and fro (for in the country itself I fared well, because I immediately found good support and could get along well), and the evil tricks of the newlanders, which they intended to play me and my family, as I shall relate hereafter, have awakened

ened the first impulse in me not to keep concealed what I knew. But the most important occasion for publishing this little book was the wretched and grievous condition of those who travel from Germany to this new land, and the outrageous and merciless proceeding of the Dutch man-dealers and their man-stealing emissaries; I mean the so-called newlanders, for they steal, as it were, German people under all manner of false pretenses, and deliver them into the hands of the great Dutch traffickers in human souls. These derive a large, and the newlanders a smaller profit from this traffic. This, I say, is the main cause why I publish this book. I had to bind myself even by a vow to do so. For before I left Pennsylvania, when it became known that I was about to return to Würtemberg, many Würtembergers, Durlachers and Palatines, of whom there are a great number there who repent and regret it while they live that they left their native country, implored me with tears and uplifted hands, and even in the name of God, to make this misery and sorrow known in Germany, so that not only the common people, but even princes and lords, might learn how they had fared, to prevent other innocent souls from leaving their fatherland, persuaded thereto by the newlanders, and from being sold into a like slavery. And

And so I vowed to the great God, and promised those people, to reveal to the people of Germany the pure truth about it, to the best of my knowledge and ability. I hope, therefore, that my beloved countrymen and all Germany will care no less to obtain accurate information as to how far it is to Pennsylvania, how long it takes to get there; what the journey costs, and besides, what hardships and dangers one has to pass through; what takes place when the people arrive well or ill in the country; how they are sold and dispersed; and finally, the nature and condition of the whole land. I relate both what is good and what is evil, and I hope, therefore, to be considered impartial and truthful by an honor-loving world.

When all this will have been read, I do not doubt that those who may still desire to go there, will remain in their fatherland, and carefully avoid this long and tedious journey and the fatalities connected with it; as such a journey involves with most a loss of their property, liberty and peace; with not a few even a loss of life, and I may well say, of the salvation of their souls.

From Würtemberg or Durlach to Holland and the open sea we count about 200 hours; from there across the sea to Old England as far as Kaupp, [Cowes] where the ships generally cast anchor

anchor before they start on the great sea-voyage, 150 hours; from there, till England is entirely lost sight of, above 100 hours; and then across the great ocean, that is from land to land, 1200 hours according to the statements of mariners; at length from the first land in Pennsylvania to Philadelphia over 40 hours. Which makes together a journey of 1700 hours or 1700 French miles.

This journey lasts from the beginning of May to the end of October, fully half a year, amid such hardships as no one is able to describe adequately with their misery.

The cause is because the Rhine-boats from Heilbronn to Holland have to pass by 36 custom-houses, at all of which the ships are examined, which is done when it suits the convenience of the custom-house officials. In the meantime the ships with the people are detained long, so that the passengers have to spend much money. The trip down the Rhine alone lasts therefore 4, 5 and even 6 weeks.

When the ships with the people come to Holland, they are detained there likewise 5 or 6 weeks. Because things are very dear there, the poor people have to spend nearly all they have during that time. Not to mention many sad accidents which occur here; having seen with my own eyes how a man, as he was about to to board the ship near Rotterdam, lost two children at once by drowning.

Both in Rotterdam and in Amsterdam the people are packed densely, like herrings so to say, in the large sea-vessels. One person receives a place of scarcely 2 feet width and 6 feet length in the bedstead, while many a ship carries four to six hundred souls; not to mention the innumerable implements, tools, provisions, water-barrels and other things which likewise occupy much space.

On account of contrary winds it takes the ships sometimes 2, 3 and 4 weeks to make the trip from Holland to Kaupp [Cowes] in England. But when the wind is good, they get there in 8 days or even sooner. Everything is examined there and the custom-duties paid, whence it comes that the ships ride there 8, 10 to 14 days and even longer at anchor, till they have taken in their full cargoes. During that time every one is compelled to spend his last remaining money and to consume his little stock of provisions which had been reserved for the sea; so that most passengers, finding themselves on the ocean where they would be in greater need of them, must greatly suffer from hunger and want. Many suffer want already on the water between Holland and Old England.

When

When the ships have for the last time weighed their anchors near the city of Kaupp [Cowes] in Old England, the real misery begins with the long voyage. For from there the ships, unless they have good wind, must often sail 8, 9, 10 to 12 weeks before they reach Philadelphia. But even with the best wind the voyage lasts 7 weeks.

But during the voyage there is on board these ships terrible misery, stench, fumes, horror, vomiting, many kinds of sea-sickness, fever, dysentery, headache, heat, constipation, boils, scurvy, cancer, mouth-rot, and the like, all of which come from old and sharply salted food and meat, also from very bad and foul water, so that many die miserably.

Add to this want of provisions, hunger, thirst, frost, heat, dampness, anxiety, want, afflictions and lamentations, together with other trouble, as e. v. the lice abound so frightfully, especially on sick people, that they can be scraped off the body. The misery reaches the climax when a gale rages for 2 or 3 nights and days, so that every one believes that the ship will go to the bottom with all human beings on board. In such a visitation the people cry and pray most piteously.

When in such a gale the sea rages and surges, so that the waves rise often like high mountains

mountains one above the other, and often tumble over the ship, so that one fears to go down with the ship; when the ship is constantly tossed from side to side by the storm and waves, so that no one can either walk, or sit, or lie, and the closely packed people in the berths are thereby tumbled over each other, both the sick and the well—it will be readily understood that many of these people, none of whom had been prepared for hardships, suffer so terribly from them that they do not survive it.

I myself had to pass through a severe illness at sea, and I best know how I felt at the time. These poor people often long for consolation, and I often entertained and comforted them with singing, praying and exhorting; and whenever it was possible and the winds and waves permitted it, I kept daily prayer-meetings with them on deck. Besides, I baptized five children in distress, because we had no ordained minister on board. I also held divine service every Sunday by reading sermons to the people; and when the dead were sunk in the water, I commended them and our souls to the mercy of God.

Among the healthy, impatience sometimes grows so great and cruel that one curses the other, or himself and the day of his birth, and sometimes come near killing each other. Misery and

and malice join each other, so that they cheat and rob one another. One always reproaches the other with having persuaded him to undertake the journey. Frequently children cry out against their parents, husbands against their wives and wives against their husbands, brothers and sisters, friends and acquaintances against each other. But most against the soul-traffickers.

Many sigh and cry: "Oh, that I were at home again, and if I had to lie in my pig-sty!" Or they say: "O God, if I only had a piece of good bread, or a good fresh drop of water." Many people whimper, sigh and cry piteously for their homes; most of them get home-sick. Many hundred people necessarily die and perish in such misery, and must be cast into the sea, which drives their relatives, or those who persuaded them to undertake the journey, to such despair that it is almost impossible to pacify and console them. In a word, the sighing and crying and lamenting on board the ship continues night and day, so as to cause the hearts even of the most hardened to bleed when they hear it.

No one can have an idea of the sufferings which women in confinement have to bear with their innocent children on board these ships. Few of this class escape with their lives; many a mother is cast into the water with her child as soon

soon as she is dead. One day, just as we had a heavy gale, a woman in our ship, who was to give birth and could not give birth under the circumstances, was pushed through a loop-hole [port-hole] in the ship and dropped into the sea, because she was far in the rear of the ship and could not be brought forward.

Children from 1 to 7 years rarely survive the voyage; and many a time parents are compelled to see their children miserably suffer and die from hunger, thirst and sickness, and then to see them cast into the water. I witnessed such misery in no less than 32 children in our ship, all of whom were thrown into the sea. The parents grieve all the more since their children find no resting-place in the earth, but are devoured by the monsters of the sea. It is a notable fact that children, who have not yet had the measles or small-pocks, generally get them on board the ship, and mostly die of them.

Often a father is separated by death from his wife and children, or mothers from their little children, or even both parents from their children; and sometimes whole families die in quick succession; so that often many dead persons lie in the berths beside the living ones, especially when contagious diseases have broken out on board the ship.

Many other accidents happen on board these ships,

ships, especially by falling, whereby people are often made cripples and can never be set right again. Some have also fallen into the ocean.

That most of the people get sick is not surprising, because, in addition to all other trials and hardships, warm food is served only three times a week, the rations being very poor and very little. Such meals can hardly be eaten, on account of being so unclean. The water which is served out on the ships is often very black, thick and full of worms, so that one cannot drink it without loathing, even with the greatest thirst. O surely, one would often give much money at sea for a piece of good bread, or a drink of good water, not to say a drink of good wine, if it were only to be had. I myself experienced that sufficiently, I am sorry to say. Toward the end we were compelled to eat the ship's biscuit which had been spoiled long ago; though in a whole biscuit there was scarcely a piece the size of a dollar that had not been full of red worms and spiders' nests. Great hunger and thirst force us to eat and drink everything; but many a one does so at the risk of his life. The sea-water cannot be drunk, because it is salt and bitter as gall. If this were not so, such a voyage could be made with less expense and without so many hardships.

At length, when, after a long and tedious voyage,

voyage, the ships come in sight of land, so that the promontories can be seen, which the people were so eager and anxious to see, all creep from below on deck to see the land from afar, and they weep for joy, and pray and sing, thanking and praising God. The sight of the land makes the people on board the ship, especially the sick and the half dead, alive again, so that their hearts leap within them; they shout and rejoice, and are content to bear their misery in patience, in the hope that they may soon reach the land in safety. But alas!

When the ships have landed at Philadelphia after their long voyage, no one is permitted to leave them except those who pay for their passage or can give good security; the others, who cannot pay, must remain on board the ships till they are purchased, and are released from the ships by their purchasers. The sick always fare the worst, for the healthy are naturally preferred and purchased first; and so the sick and wretched must often remain on board in front of the city for 2 or 3 weeks, and frequently die, whereas many a one, if he could pay his debt and were permitted to leave the ship immediately, might recover and remain alive.

Before I describe how this traffic in human flesh is conducted, I must mention how much the

the journey to Philadelphia or Pennsylvania costs.

A person over 10 years pays for the passage from Rotterdam to Philadelphia 10 pounds, or 60 florins. Children from 5 to 10 years pay half price, 5 pounds or 30 florins. All children under 5 years are free. For these prices the passengers are conveyed to Philadelphia, and, as long as they are at sea, provided with food, though with very poor, as has been shown above.

But this is only the sea-passage; the other costs on land, from home to Rotterdam, including the passage on the Rhine, are at least 40 florins, no matter how economically one may live. No account is here taken of extraordinary contingencies. I may safely assert that, with the greatest economy, many passengers have spent 200 florins from home to Philadelphia.

The sale of human beings in the market on board the ship is carried on thus: Every day Englishmen, Dutchmen and High-German people come from the city of Philadelphia and other places, in part from a great distance, say 20, 30, or 40 hours away, and go on board the newly arrived ship that has brought and offers for sale passengers from Europe, and select among the healthy persons such as they deem suitable for their business, and bargain with them how long they will serve for their passage money, which
most

most of them are still in debt for. When they have come to an agreement, it happens that adult persons bind themselves in writing to serve 3, 4, 5 or 6 years for the amount due by them, according to their age and strength. But very young people, from 10 to 15 years, must serve till they are 21 years old.

Many parents must sell and trade away their children like so many head of cattle; for if their children take the debt upon themselves, the parents can leave the ship free and unrestrained; but as the parents often do not know where and to what people their children are going, it often happens that such parents and children, after leaving the ship, do not see each other again for many years, perhaps no more in all their lives.

When people arrive who cannot make themselves free, but have children under 5 years, the parents cannot free themselves by them; for such children must be given to somebody without compensation to be brought up, and they must serve for their bringing up till they are 21 years old. Children from 5 to 10 years, who pay half price for their passage, viz. 30 florins, must likewise serve for it till they are 21 years of age; they cannot, therefore, redeem their parents by taking the debt of the latter upon themselves. But children above 10 years can take

take part of their parents' debt upon themselves.

A woman must stand for her husband if he arrives sick, and in like manner a man for his sick wife, and take the debt upon herself or himself, and thus serve 5 to 6 years not alone for his or her own debt, but also for that of the sick husband or wife. But if both are sick, such persons are sent from the ship to the sick-house [hospital], but not until it appears probable that they will find no purchasers. As soon as they are well again they must serve for their passage, or pay if they have means.

It often happens that whole families, husband, wife, and children, are separated by being sold to different purchasers, especially when they have not paid any part of their passage money.

When a husband or wife has died at sea, when the ship has made more than half of her trip, the survivor must pay or serve not only for himself or herself, but also for the deceased.

When both parents have died over half-way at sea, their children, especially when they are young and have nothing to pawn or to pay, must stand for their own and their parents' passage, and serve till they are 21 years old. When one has served his or her term, he or she is entitled to a new suit of clothes at parting; and if it has been so stipulated, a man gets in addition a horse, a woman, a cow.

When

When a serf has an opportunity to marry in this country, he or she must pay for each year which he or she would have yet to serve, 5 to 6 pounds. But many a one who has thus purchased and paid for his bride, has subsequently repented his bargain, so that he would gladly have returned his exorbitantly dear ware, and lost the money besides.

If some one in this country runs away from his master, who has treated him harshly, he cannot get far. Good provision has been made for such cases, so that a runaway is soon recovered. He who detains or returns a deserter receives a good reward.

If such a runaway has been away from his master one day, he must serve for it as a punishment a week, for a week a month, and for a month half a year. But if the master will not keep the runaway after he has got him back, he may sell him for so many years as he would have to serve him yet.

Work and labor in this new and wild land are very hard and manifold, and many a one who came there in his old age must work very hard to his end for his bread. I will not speak of young people. Work mostly consists in cutting wood, felling oak-trees, rooting out, or as they say there, clearing large tracts of forest. Such forests, being cleared, are then laid out for

for fields and meadows. From the best hewn wood, fences are made around the new fields; for there all meadows, orchards and fruit-fields, are surrounded and fenced in with planks made of thickly-split wood, laid one above the other, as in zigzag lines, and within such enclosures, horses, cattle, and sheep, are permitted to graze. Our Europeans, who are purchased, must always work hard, for new fields are constantly laid out; and so they learn that stumps of oak-trees are in America certainly as hard as in Germany. In this hot land they fully experience in their own persons what God has imposed on man for his sin and disobedience; for in Genesis we read the words: In the sweat of thy brow shalt thou eat bread. Who therefore wishes to earn his bread in a Christian and honest way, and cannot earn it in his fatherland otherwise than by the work of his hands, let him do so in his own country, and not in America; for he will not fare better in America. However hard he may be compelled to work in his fatherland, he will surely find it quite as hard, if not harder, in the new country. Besides, there is not only the long and arduous journey lasting half a year, during which he has to suffer, more than with the hardest work; he has also spent about 200 florins which no one will refund to him. If he has so much money, it will slip out of his hands;

hands; if he has it not, he must work his debt off as a slave and poor serf. Therefore let every one stay in his own country and support himself and his family honestly. Besides I say that those who suffer themselves to be persuaded and enticed away by the man-thieves, are very foolish if they believe that roasted pigeons will fly into their mouths in America or Pennsylvania without their working for them.

How miserably and wretchedly so many thousand German families have fared, 1) since they lost all their cash means in consequence of the long and tedious journey; 2) because many of them died miserably and were thrown into the water; 3) because, on account of their great poverty, most of these families after reaching the land are separated from each other and sold far away from each other, the young and the old. And the saddest of all this is that parents must generally give away their minor children without receiving a compensation for them; inasmuch as such children never see or meet their fathers, mothers, brothers or sisters again, and as many of them are not raised in any Christian faith by the people to whom they are given.

For there are many doctrines of faith and sects in Pennsylvania which cannot all be enumerated, because many a one will not confess to what faith he belongs.

Besides,

Besides, there are many hundreds of adult persons who have not been and do not even wish to be baptized. There are many who think nothing of the sacraments and the Holy Bible, nor even of God and his word. Many do not even believe that there is a true God and devil, a heaven and a hell, salvation and damnation, a resurrection of the dead, a judgment and an eternal life; they believe that all one can see is natural. For in Pennsylvania every one may not only believe what he will, but he may even say it freely and openly.

Consequently, when young persons, not yet grounded in religion, come to serve for many years with such free-thinkers and infidels, and are not sent to any church or school by such people, especially when they live far from any school or church. Thus it happens that such innocent souls come to no true divine recognition, and grow up like heathens and Indians.

A voyage is sometimes dangerous to people, who bring money or goods away with them from home, because much is spoiled at sea by entering sea-water; sometimes they are even robbed on board the ship by dishonest people; so that such formerly opulent persons find themselves in a most deplorable condition.

A sad example of a Würtemberger shall be mentioned here. In the autumn of A. D. 1753

a

a certain Daser of Nagold arrived with his wife and 8 children in a wretched and unfortunate situation at Philadelphia in Pennsylvania. For not only was he robbed at sea of goods worth 1800 florins, but he had on that account a long law-suit with the English captain of the ship at Philadelphia, which suit, however, he did not win, but had even to pay the cost of the litigation. Mr. Daser had to pay 600 florins for his own passage and that of his family. But as he had been robbed of his money, all his goods and chattels together with the boxes were sold at public auction or vendue for a trifling sum, so that he became more and more distressed with his family. Then, as he proceeded to borrow money to purchase a plantation, he was shamefully cheated by his creditor. He had agreed with him to repay the borrowed money in two years; but the person who made out the obligation or bond, as they call it there, wrote at the instigation of the unscrupulous creditor *in two days*, instead of *in two years*. Mr. Daser signed this, never suspecting that he signed his own ruin, because he did not understand English. The result was that, as he did not repay the money in two days (N. B. He had not ever received the money, the time having expired in consequence of his own negligence and various idle pretenses of the creditor), all that he still called

called his own was sold and even taken away from his body. He would even have been sent to prison, or been compelled to sell his children, had he not been saved by my intercession by Captain Von Diemer, who always had a kind and tender regard for Germans. Said Captain Von Diemer provided Mr. Daser and his family for mercy's sake until the end of his litigation with victuals, money, beds and shelter, at the same time giving security for him, so that Mr. Daser remained free from the debtors' prison. Before my departure Captain Von Diemer promised Mr. Daser and me with hand and mouth that, as long as he lived, he would help provide for the Daser family and their needs. Mr. Daser dined with us 8 weeks and slept with me, but his many sad reverses have made him quite desponding and half crazy. Shortly before my departure his two oldest daughters and his oldest son were compelled to bind themselves in writing to serve 3 years each.

I avail myself of this opportunity to relate a few remarkable and most disastrous cases of shipwrecks. In the year 1754, on St. James' day, a ship with some 360 souls on board, mostly Wurtembergers, Durlachers and Palatines, was hurled by a gale in the night upon a rock between Holland and Old England. It received three shocks, each accompanied by a tremendous crash,

crash, and finally it split lengthwise asunder at the bottom, so that the water entered, which rose so fast that the ship began to sink early in the morning. At the last extremity, when the people endeavored to save themselves, 63 persons sprang into a boat. But as this boat was too overburdened, and another person reached it by swimming, holding persistently on to it, it was not possible to drive him away till they chopped his hands off, when he went down. Another person, in order to save himself, jumped on a barrel which had fallen out of the large ship, but which immediately capsized and sank with him. But the passengers in the large ship held on partly to the rigging, partly to the masts; many of them stood deep in the water, beat their hands together above their heads and raised an indescribably piteous hue and cry. As the boat steered away, its occupants saw the large ship with 300 souls on board sink to the bottom before their eyes. But the merciful God sent those who had saved themselves in the boat, an English ship that had been sailing near, and which took the poor shipwrecks on board and brought them back to the land. This great disaster would never have been known in Germany if the ship had gone down during the night with all its human freight on board.

The following fatal voyage, where all the passengers,

sengers were Germans, has probably not become known in Germany at all. In the year 1752 a ship arrived at Philadelphia which was fully six months at sea from Holland to Philadelphia. This ship had weathered many storms throughout the winter and could not reach the land; finally another ship came to the assistance of the half-wrecked and starved vessel. Of about 340 souls this ship brought 21 persons to Philadelphia, who stated that they had not only spent fully six months at sea, and had been driven by the storm to the coast of Ireland, but that most of the passengers had died by starvation, that they had lost their masts and sails, captain and mates, and that the rest would never have reached the land if God had not sent another ship to their aid which brought them to the land.

There is another case of a lost ship that has probably never been made known in Germany. That ship sailed a few years ago with almost exclusively German passengers, from Holland to Philadelphia, but nothing was ever heard of it except that a notice was afterward sent from Holland to the merchants of Philadelphia. Such cases of entirely lost and shipwrecked vessels are not reported to Germany, for fear that it might deter the people from emigrating and induce them to stay at home.

I cannot possibly pass over in silence what was reported to me by a reliable person in Pennsylvania, in a package of letters which left Philadelphia Dec. 10, 1754, and came to my hands Sept. 1, 1755. These letters lament the fact that last autumn, A. D. 1754, to the very great burden of the country, more than 22,000 souls (there was a great emigration from Würtemberg at that time) had arrived in Philadelphia alone, mostly Würtembergers, Palatines, Durlachers and Swiss, who had been so wretchedly sick and poor that most of these people had been obliged to sell their children on account of their great poverty. The country, so the letters state, had been seriously molested by this great mass of people, especially by the many sick people, many of whom were still daily filling the graves.

So long as I was there, from 20 to 24 ships with passengers arrived at Philadelphia alone every autumn, which amounted in 4 years to more than 25,000 souls, exclusive of those who died at sea or since they left home, and without counting those ships which sailed with their passengers to other English colonies, as New York, Boston, Maryland, Nova Scotia and Carolina, whereby these colonies were filled, and the immigrants became very unwelcome, especially in the city of Philadelphia. But that so so many people emigrate to America, and particularly to Pennsylvania, is due to the deceptions and persuasions practised by the so-called newlanders,

These men-thieves inveigle people of every rank and profession, among them many soldiers, scholars, artists and mechanics. They rob the princes and lords of their subjects and take them to Rotterdam or Amsterdam to be sold there. They receive there from their merchants for every person of 10 years and over, 3 florins or a ducat; whereas the merchants get in Philadelphia 60, 70 or 80 florins for such a person, in proportion as said person has incurred more or less debts during the voyage. When such a newlander has collected a "transport," and if it does not suit him to accompany them to America, he stays behind, passes the winter in Holland or elsewhere; in the spring he obtains again money in advance for emigrants from his merchants, goes to Germany again, pretending that he had come from Pennsylvania with the intention of purchasing all sorts of merchandise which he was going to take there.

Frequently these newlanders say that they had received power-of-attorney from some countrymen or from the authorities of Pennsylvania to obtain legacies or inheritances for these countrymen; and that they would avail themselves

themselves of this good and sure opportunity to take their friends, brothers or sisters, or even their parents with them; and it has often happened that such old people followed them, trusting to the persuasion of these newlanders that they would be better provided for.

Such old people they seek to get away with them in order to entice other people to follow them. Thus they have seduced many away who said that if such and such relatives of theirs went to America, they would risk it too. These men-thieves resort to various tricks, never forgetting to display their money before the poor people, but which is nothing else but a bait from Holland and accursed blood-money.

When these men-thieves persuade persons of rank, such as nobles, learned or skilled people, who cannot pay their passage and cannot give security, these are treated just like ordinary poor people, and must remain on board the ship till some one comes and buys them from the captain. And when they are released at last from the ship, they must serve their lords and masters, by whom they have been bought, like common day-laborers. Their rank, skill and learning avails them nothing, for here none but laborers and mechanics are wanted. But the worst is that such people, who are not accustomed to work, are treated to blows and cuffs,

cuffs, like cattle, till they have learned the hard work. Many a one, on finding himself thus shamefully deceived by the newlanders, has shortened his own life, or has given way to despair, so that he could not be helped, or has run away, only to fare worse afterwards than before.

It often happens that the merchants in Holland make a secret contract with their captains and the newlanders, to the effect that the latter must take the ships with their human freight to another place in America, and not to Pennsylvania where these people want to go, if they think that they can elsewhere find a better market for them. Many a one who has a good friend or acquaintance, or a relative in Pennsylvania, to whose helping care he has trusted, finds himself thus grievously disappointed in consequence of such infamous deception, being separated from friends whom he will never see again either in this or in that country. Thus emigrants are compelled in Holland to submit to the wind and to the captain's will, because they cannot know at sea where the ship is steered to. But all this is the fault of the newlanders and of some unscrupulous dealers in human flesh in Holland.

Many people who go to Philadelphia entrust their money, which they have brought with them

them from home, to these newlanders. But these thieves often remain in Holland with the money, or sail from there with another ship to another English colony, so that the poor defrauded people, when they reach the country, have no other choice but to serve or to sell their children, if they have any, only to get away from the ship.

The following remarkable case may serve as an example. In 1753, a noble lady, N. V., came with her two half-grown daughters and a young son to Philadelphia. On the trip down the Rhine she entrusted more than 1000 rix-dollars to a newlander who was well known to her. But when the ship, on which the lady had taken passage, started from Holland, this villain remained behind with the money; in consequence of which the lady found herself in such want and distress that her two daughters were compelled to serve. In the following spring this poor lady sent her son to Holland to search for the embezzler of her money; but at the time of my departure, A. D. 1754, nothing had been heard of him as yet, and it was even rumored that the young gentleman had died during his voyage.

It is impossible, however, to discuss all these circumstances; besides I am sure that the newlanders and men-thieves, on coming to Germany,

many, never reveal the truth about these wretched voyages full of dangers and hardships.

Frequently many letters are entrusted in Pennsylvania and other English colonies to newlanders who return to the old country. When they get to Holland, they have these letters opened, or they open them themselves, and if any one has written the truth, his letter is either rewritten so as to suit the purpose of these harpies, or simply destroyed. While in Pennsylvania, I myself heard such men-thieves say that there were Jews enough in Holland, ready to furnish them for a small consideration counterfeits of any seal, and who could perfectly forge any handwriting. They can imitate all characters, marks and tokens so admirably that even he whose handwriting they have imitated must acknowledge it to be his own. By means of such practices they deceive even people who are not credulous, thus playing their nefarious tricks in a covert manner. They say to their confidants that this is the best way to induce the people to emigrate. I myself came very near being deceived.

Some great merchants in Holland attempted not to let me continue my journey home, but to induce me by stratagem or force to return to England and America. For they not only told me verbally in Rotterdam, but even tried to prove

prove to me by writing from Amsterdam, that my wife and child, together with my sister-in-law and many countrymen, had embarked for Philadelphia with the last transport last summer. They told me very accurately the names of my wife and child, how old and tall they were, and that my wife had said her husband had been an organist in Pennsylvania for four years; they also showed me my wife's name in a letter, and told me with what ship and captain had sailed from Amsterdam, and that my wife was lodged with four other women in berth No. 22, which circumstantial communication had the effect of making one exceedingly confused and irresolute. But I read to them letters from my wife in which she plainly said that she would never in all her life go there without me, on the contrary that she eagerly awaited my return. I said that I had written to her again that I had made up my mind to return, God willing, to Germany next year, wherefore I could not possibly believe all this. The merchants then produced witnesses, which made me so perplexed that I did not know what to believe or to do. At length, however, after mature deliberation, and no doubt by divine direction, I came to the conclusion that, inasmuch as I had already the greater part of my arduous journey, viz. 1400 hours way, behind me, and had arrived at the

borders

borders of Germany, I would now in God's name continue and finish my journey, which I did, and thus, thanks to the Most High, I have escaped this great temptation. For I came to see that all that I had been told and shown in Holland with respect to my family had been untrue, as I found my wife and child safe at home. If I had believed those seducers of the people, and had returned to England and America, not only would this account of my journey not have been published so soon, but I should, perhaps, never have met my family again in this world. Those frequently mentioned men-thieves, as I subsequently learned, gave an accurate account of me and my wife to the merchants in Holland, and the newlanders tried a second time to persuade my wife to follow them. The merchants no doubt thought that, if I returned home, I should reveal their whole nefarious traffic and the deplorable condition of the numerous families that emigrated and rushed into their ruin, and that I should thereby cause great damage to their shipping interests and their traffic in human flesh.

I must state here something that I have forgotten above. As soon as the ships that bring passengers from Europe have cast their anchors in the port of Philadelphia, all male persons of 15 years and upward are placed on the following

ing morning into a boat and led two by two to the court-house or town-hall of the city. There they must take the oath of allegiance to the Crown of Great Britain. This being done, they are taken in the same manner back to the ships. Then the traffic in human souls begins, as related above. I only add that in purchasing these people no one asks for references as to good character or an honorable discharge. If any one had escaped the gallows, and had the rope still dangling around his neck, or if he had left both his ears in Europe, nothing would be put in his way in Pennsylvania. But if he is again caught in wrong-doing, he is hopelessly lost. For gallows' birds and wheel candidates, Pennsylvania is, therefore, a desirable land.

DESCRIPTION

DESCRIPTION OF THE LAND PENNSYLVANIA.

PENNSYLVANIA is one of the English settlements or colonies in North America. It borders on the sea, and is just in the centre between the other English plantation lands. Far above it, in the north, are Nova Scotia, New England, New York, and New Jersey; below it, in the south, Maryland, Virginia, Carolina, and Georgia. From the city of London to the point where we lose Old England out of sight we count 325 English miles; then, from land to land, that is from the last land in Old England to the first land in Pennsylvania 3600 such miles, from there to Philadelphia 125 miles, which makes together 4050 English miles, or 1350 German or rather Swabian hours. 3 English miles make a Swabian hour, but 25 such hours make a degree, just as the French land miles. When the ships come near this land, they sail from the ocean into the great river. This is a large bay formed by the Delaware River, or rather, it is the

the Delaware River itself which is very broad here. On the way to Philadelphia one sees on both sides a large flat land with woods here and there. The passage from the sea, and the entrance into the great river is in a northwesterly direction. The Delaware River separates below at the entrance, the two colonies, Pennsylvania and Maryland, from each other, Maryland to the left, Pennsylvania to the right. While on the river, we can see much high mountain land, especially the Blue Mountains, and on the left hand the tall and exceedingly beautiful cedar trees. At the entrance from the sea the river is so broad that we can scarcely see the land on either side. It grows gradually narrower, and at Philadelphia the Delaware is about half an hour wide. Here the river has twice every 24 hours ebb and flow from the sea. This city lies, as above stated, 125 English miles or 40 hours journey from the open sea, higher up in the land, hard by said river into which most of the rivers of this colony empty; the other waters flow into the other great main river of Pennsylvania, which is called Susquehanna, and empties into the Chesapeake Bay. In Philadelphia we can see the open sea through a field-glass.

Said city is the capital of Pennsylvania where all the commerce is carried on. It is already very

very large, regularly and handsomely built, and laid out with broad streets and many cross-alleys. All the houses are built of stone or brick up to the fourth story, and roofed with shingles of cedar wood. It takes almost a day to walk around the town; about 300 new houses are built every year. It is thought that in time it will be one of the largest cities in the world. The principal language and the law of the land is English. It has no walls nor ramparts, these being deemed unnecessary. On two sides the city has navigable waters, toward morning the above mentioned Delaware, and toward midnight the Schuylkill River, both of which join below the city. Many large and small merchant-vessels are built there near the water. The trade of the city and country to other countries and colonies increases perceptibly from year to year; it consists in fruit, flour, corn, tobacco, honey, skins, various kinds of costly furs, flax, and particularly a great deal of flax-seed or linseed, also fine cut lumber, horses, and all kinds of tame and wild animals. In return the incoming vessels bring all sorts of goods, such as Spanish, Portuguese and German wines, the best of which cost a rix-dollar, the most inferior a florin per quart. Also spices, sugar, tea, coffee, rice, rum, which is a brandy distilled from sugar, molasses

molasses, fine china vessels, Dutch and English cloths, leather, linen, stuffs, silks, damask, velvet, etc. There is actually everything to be had in Pennsylvania that may be obtained in Europe, because so many merchantmen land here every year. Ships are coming from Holland, Old and New England, Scotland, Ireland, Spain, Portugal, Maryland, New York, Carolina, and from the West and East Indies. By "West Indies" the people of Pennsylvania mean the Spanish and Portuguese America, and also the American Islands, whether they belong to the English or to other nations.

In Philadelphia there is a new and splendid court or town house, which is very high and has four doors and four entrances. It is 100 feet long and 100 feet wide, stands free, and has tall English plate [glass] windows. In this town there are already eight churches, three English, three German, one Swedish, and one Quaker church. In the last named one can often hear and see a woman preach in English, but no singing is heard in this class [sect], because they don't believe in singing. After the sermon is over, he who has objections against the sermon steps forth and explains his opinion; and then one can often hear two persons disputing before the whole assemblage, which lasts sometimes longer than the sermon.

A

A *gymnasium* [college] has also been established in the city, where several languages are taught; for in this city and country people from every part of the world can be seen, especially Europeans, of whom one could count more than a hundred thousand. The Germans are most numerous among the inhabitants of Pennsylvania. Many of these Germans study diverse languages in said *gymnasium*.

In the court house of Philadelphia, four principal courts are annually held, and public judgment is passed in all occurring cases. Young and old may enter the court-room on such court-days and hear what is tried and transacted, and which often gives rise to a terrible laughter among the audience.

I will quote here but one example out of many. One day the following case was tried in the court: An unmarried woman, who had suffered herself to be got with child, and who wanted the man who was responsible for her condition to marry her, stated that he had forced her to the act. Both parties being summoned and heard, the defendant in the case would neither hear nor answer, but looked rigidly and immovably at the gentlemen *Assimle* [gentlemen of the Assembly, *i. e.*, judges], no matter what they said and asked, he having been instructed to act thus by his lawyer. After they had

had tried it with him long enough, and when he was to go to prison, which was shouted aloud into his ear, he suddenly recovered his hearing. He excused himself, asked pardon, and said that when he forced the woman she screamed so terribly that he lost his hearing. But the woman started up and said: O, you godless rogue, how can you say so? I did not speak a word at that time. Which he admitted, and said that was true, he only wanted this confession from her. And why did she not cry? There had been people enough sleeping in the house that night. Whereupon she replied, if she had thought that she would get with child this time she would surely have cried for help. This called forth loud laughter among the young and old, and the defendant was acquitted of the charge against him.

I will here quote another story which did not turn out so favorably for the man implicated in it. A purchased woman servant in an English house became pregnant by her master's purchased man servant. Being no longer able to conceal her condition, she reported it to her master, who was a *Justice*, which means as much as a judge or alderman. The master who was very angry over this lapse, said at last, from compassion with her: She would do herself a great wrong if she charged that loose

loose bird with being the father of her child;
for in the first place his time of serving would
not expire before a long time yet, and then he
did not call a farthing his own, and besides she
knew herself that he was a spendthrift and
would never be able to support her and her
child. But if she would follow him he would
give her better advice, so that she and her
child would be provided for in the future. The
afflicted woman was very anxious to know it,
and promised her master to follow his advice,
entreating him to tell her wherein it consisted.
Her master then warned her earnestly not to
betray him, and told her to go to another *Justice*, because he as her master might be considered too partial in this case, and charge another
unmarried man, whose name and good circumstances were well known to her, with being the
father of her child; but she must stand to it
[stick to it or, swear to it]. This advice
pleased the woman quite well; but on further
consideration she went to another *Justice*, revealed her condition to him and stated that her
master himself was the father of her child, and
that she could stand to it, although her master
would not confess it; being a widower, he could
and should keep her now. The *Justice* then
administered the oath to her according to the
English law; this is done by kissing the Bible.
As

As soon as this was done he sent a constable for her master, this is customary in the land, and subjected him to a hearing. But as he would not confess, he had to go to prison and stay there so long till he promised in writing either to marry his pregnant servant woman or to pay her 200 pounds, which is 1200 florins in German money. Under such circumstances he chose to marry his servant woman, rather than give her 1200 florins. He himself acknowledged this as right and just, because he had advised her to charge an innocent man with being the father of her child. He was married to her on the spot. Such and similar cases happen frequently in that country, mainly because the women enjoy such great liberties and privileges.

Coming to speak of Pennsylvania again, that colony possesses great liberties above all other English colonies, inasmuch as all religious sects are tolerated there. We find there Lutherans, Reformed, Catholics, Quakers, Mennonists or Anabaptists, Herrnhuters or Moravian Brethren, Pietists, Seventh Day Baptists, Dunkers, Presbyterians, Newborn, Freemasons, Separatists, Freethinkers, Jews, Mohammedans, Pagans, Negroes and Indians. The Evangelicals and Reformed, however, are in the majority. But there are many hundred unbaptized souls

souls there that do not even wish to be baptized. Many pray neither in the morning nor in the evening, neither before nor after meals. No devotional book, not to speak of a Bible, will be found with such people. In one house and one family, 4, 5, and even 6 sects, may be found.

Liberty in Pennsylvania extends so far that every one is free from all molestation and taxation on his property, business, house and estates. On a hundred acres of land a tax of no more than an English shilling is paid annually, which is called ground-rent or quit-rent; a shilling is about 18 kreuzers of German money. A peculiarity, however, is that unmarried men and women pay from 2 to 5 shillings annually, according to their income, because they have no one but themselves to provide for. In Philadelphia this money is applied to the purchase of the lights which burn every night in the streets of the city.

This country was granted by the King of England to a distinguished Quaker named PENN, from whom the land of Pennsylvania takes its name. Even now there are some young Lords Von PENN who, however, do not reside in the country, but in London, in Old England. A. D. 1754, a young Lord Von PENN was in the country. He renewed and confirmed

firmed all the former liberties with his signature, and made many presents to the Indians or savages.

No trade or profession in Pennsylvania is bound by guilds; every one may carry on whatever business he will or can, and if any one could or would carry on ten trades, no one would have a right to prevent him; and if, for instance, a lad as an apprentice, or through his own unaided exertions, learns his art or trade in six months, he can pass for a master, and may marry whenever he chooses. It is a surprising fact that young people who were born in this new land, are very clever, docile and skilful; for many a one looks at a work of skill or art only a few times, and imitates it immediately, while in Germany many a one has to learn for years to do the same thing perfectly. But here many a one is able to produce the most artful things in a short time. When the young folks have gone to school for six months, they are generally able to read anything.

The land of Pennsylvania is a healthy land; it has for the most part good soil, good air and water, many high mountains, and also much flat land; it is very rich in wood; where it is not inhabited a pure forest in which many small and large waters flow. The land is also very fertile, and all sorts of grain grow well. It is quite populous,

populous, too, inhabited far and wide, and several new towns have been founded here and there, as Philadelphia, Germantown, Lancaster, Rittengstaun [Reading], Bethlehem, and New-Frankfurt [Frankford]. There are also many churches built in the country; but many people have to go a journey of 2, 3, 4, 5 to 10 hours to get to church; but all people, men and women, ride to church on horseback, though they had only half an hour to walk, which is customary also at funerals and weddings. Sometimes one can count at such country weddings and funerals 300, 400, and even 500 persons on horseback. It may be readily imagined that on such occasions, as also at the holy communion, no one appears in black clothes, crapes, or cloaks.

I will give a somewhat more detailed account of the funeral customs. When some one has died, especially in the country, where on account of the intervening plantations and forests people live far from one another, the time appointed for the funeral is always indicated only to the 4 nearest neighbors; each of these in his turn notifies his own nearest neighbor. In this manner such an invitation to a funeral is made known more than fifty English miles around in 24 hours. If it is possible, one or more persons from each house appear on horseback at the appointed time to attend the funeral. While the

the people are coming in, good cake cut into pieces is handed around on a large tin platter to those present; each person receives then in a goblet, a hot West India Rum punch, into which lemon, sugar and juniper berries are put, which give it a delicious taste. After this, hot and sweetened cider is served. This custom at the funeral assemblies in America is just the same as that at the wedding gatherings in Europe. When the people have nearly all assembled, and the time for the burial has come, the dead body is carried to the general burial-place, or where that is too far away, the deceased is buried in his own field. The assembled people ride all in silence behind the coffin, and sometimes one can count from 100 to 500 persons on horseback. The coffins are all made of fine walnut wood and stained brown with a shining varnish. Well-to-do people have four finely-wrought brass handles attached to the coffin, by which the latter is held and carried to the grave. If the deceased person was a young man, the body is carried to the grave by four maidens, while that of a deceased maiden is carried by four unmarried men.

It is no unusual thing in this country to hear a totally unlearned man preaching in the open field, for the sectarians say and believe that the scholars of the present day are no longer apostles,

apostles, and that they are only making a trade of their learning. Nevertheless, there are many excellent preachers in Pennsylvania who, by the grace of God and by their indefatigable toil, have converted many souls to the Christian faith; I myself have witnessed how our evangelical ministers have baptized and confirmed many adult persons, both white and black. Such an act is always attended by a large concourse of people. But I am sorry to say that there are also quite unworthy preachers who give offence to many people, and who furnish the sectarians with arguments, to the great annoyance of our ministers. I will quote here an example of such an objectionable preacher. One by the name of Alexander, of Oley township, said in a meeting of young farmers, with whom he had been drinking and carousing, that he would preach so that all his hearers who stood in front of him would weep, but those that stood behind him must all laugh. To this effect he bet a considerable sum with said young farmers. On the appointed day he appeared at a church-meeting, took his stand in the middle of the people, and began to hold a touching and pathetic sermon. Seeing that his hearers were moved to tears, he put his hands behind him, drew his coat-tails asunder, exhibiting a pair of badly-torn breeches through which his

his bare posterior, which he scratched with one hand, shone forth, so that those who stood behind him could not help roaring with laughter. Thus he had won his wager. This disgusting affair was published in the English and German newspapers of Philadelphia. The sectarians said often to those of our own faith that such men were the false prophets that went about in sheep's clothing, but were in fact rapacious wolves. But this is a source of great annoyance and vexation to all righteous teachers and good pastors.

There are at present many good English, Swedish, Dutch and German preachers of the Lutheran and the Reformed churches in Pennsylvania, of whom the following are very well known to me. Among the English, the three brothers TENNENT and Mr. DATT. Three Swedish ministers who are very closely associated with our preachers and hold yearly conferences with them. But the German Evangelical Lutheran preachers are: Mr. MÜHLENBERG, senior, in Providence township and New Hanover. Mr. BRUNHOLZ, in Philadelphia. Mr. HANDSCHUH, in Germantown. Mr. KURZ, in Tulpehocken. Mr. WAGNER, in Readingstoun (Reading). Mr. HEINZELMANN, in Philadelphia. Mr. SCHULZ, Mr. WEYGAND, Mr. SCHRENK, Mr. SCHARTEL, in the Blue Mountains. Mr. HART-
WICH,

wich, in New York. Mr. Görack, in Lancaster. Reformed ministers are; Mr. Schlatter, Mr. Steiner, Mr. Siebele, Mr. Weiss, Mr. Michael, Mr. Streitter, and Mr. Laidig, without mentioning the Dutch and others whose names are not known to me.

The preachers in Pennsylvania receive no salaries or tithes, except what they annually get from their church members, which varies very much; for many a father of a family gives according to his means and of his own free will 2, 3, 4, 5 or 6 florins a year, but many others give very little. For baptizing children, for funeral sermons and marriage ceremonies they generally receive a dollar. The preachers have no free dwellings or other *beneficia*. But they receive many presents from their parishioners. The same is true of the schoolmasters. But since 1754 England and Holland give annually a large sum of money for the general benefit of the many poor in Pennsylvania, and for the support of 6 Reformed English churches and as many Reformed English free schools. Nevertheless, many hundred children cannot attend these schools, on account of their great distance and the many forests. Many planters lead, therefore, a very wild and heathenish life; for as it is with the schools, so it is also with the churches in the rural districts, because churches and

and school-houses are usually built around at such places only, where most neighbors and church members live.*

The preachers throughout Pennsylvania have no power to punish any one, or to compel any one to go to church; nor has any one a right

---

* In an English publication, which treats of the condition of the immigrants who have settled in Pennsylvania, Virginia, Maryland, etc., the following is reported among other things: From the most trustworthy accounts which we have of these provinces, it appears that the number of immigrants there has increased exceedingly within the last few years. They consist for the most part of Palatines, Franconians, and Swiss. In the Colony of Pennsylvania alone there are over 100,000; of these about 20,000 belong to the Reformed, nearly as many to the Lutheran, and about 1700 to the Roman Catholic religion. The rest consists of Anabaptists, Moravians, Brethren of Zion, Rondorfers, and other Separatists. As among the latter almost every one is his own teacher, it may be said of them that they have their tenets (if the inanities of these people may be called so) better by heart than many of the other denominations; for although not a few pious and illumined Christians may be found among the latter, by far the majority live in the deepest ignorance, which must be ascribed to the want of sufficient preachers and schoolmasters, the inhabitants lacking the means for their support. The author of this publication closes with the wish that the nation of Great Britain might duly consider the condition of their brethren, both in a spiritual and worldly aspect, and do for them what is necessary to have in them a constant bulwark in America against all their enemies.

to dictate to the other, because they are not supported by any *Consistorio*. Most preachers are hired by the year like the cowherds in Germany; and if one does not preach to their liking, he must expect to be served with a notice that his services will no longer be required. It is, therefore, very difficult to be a conscientious preacher, especially as they have to hear and suffer much from so many hostile and often wicked sects. The most exemplary preachers are often reviled, insulted and scoffed at like the Jews, by the young and old, especially in the country I would, therefore, rather perform the meanest herdsman's duties in Germany than be a preacher in Pennsylvania. Such unheard-of rudeness and wickedness spring from the excessive liberties of the land, and from the blind zeal of the many sects. To many a one's soul and body, liberty in Pennsylvania is more hurtful than useful. There is a saying in that country: Pennsylvania is the heaven of the farmers, the paradise of the mechanics, and the hell of the officials and preachers.

The Governor in my time, had his residence in Philadelphia, his name was Hamilton. Every 6 years a new Governor is elected by the King and Parliament of England, and sent there to govern in the name of the King; but the land

land and most of the revenues belong to a Quaker by the name of Penn, hence also the city of Philadelphia and the land are densely peopled by Quakers.

Provisions are cheap in Pennsylvania, but everything that is manufactured and brought into the country is three or four times as dear as in Germany. Wood, salt and sugar, excepted. Otherwise we can purchase in Germany as much with one florin as here with 4 or 5 florins. Nevertheless, the people live well, especially on all sorts of grain, which thrives very well, because the soil is wild and fat. They grow chiefly rye, wheat, barley, oats, buckwheat, corn, flax, hemp, fruit, cabbage and turnips. They also have good cattle, fast horses, and many bees. The sheep, which are larger than the German ones, have generally two lambs a year. Hogs and poultry, especially turkeys, are raised by almost everybody. In this country the chickens are not put in houses by night, nor are they looked after; but they sit summer and winter upon the trees near the houses; every evening many a tree is so full of chickens that the boughs bend beneath them. The poultry is in no danger from beasts of prey, because every plantation owner has a big dog, if not more, at large around his house.

Even in the humblest and poorest houses in this

this country there is no meal without meat, and no one eats the bread without butter or cheese, although the bread is as good as with us. It is very annoying, however, that nothing but salt meat is eaten in summer, and rarely fresh meat in winter.

On account of the extensive stock-raising, meat is very cheap; one can buy the best beef for 3 kreuzers a pound, pork and mutton for 2 kreuzers and 3 hellers. Besides, one can buy at the market of Philadelphia many kinds of meat, venison, poultry, fish and birds, as one chooses, for very little money. I don't think that there is any country in which more meat is eaten and consumed than in Pennsylvania. The English know little or nothing of soup eating; bread and butter and cheese are always their dessert, and because sugar, tea and coffee, are very cheap, they drink coffee and the like 2 or 3 times daily. The common sugar costs 10 kr. a pound, the best 15 kr. Coffee is of the same price; rice costs 3 kr. a pound. Vegetables of every description are raised in abundance. A bushel of salt can be bought for 15 kr., and timber and wood for fuel every one has for nothing. Market is held twice a week in Philadelphia; it always attracts a great concourse of people. The ordinary meat stalls which are over 100 feet long, hang on both sides

sides full of all kinds of meat, which is always bought up and consumed by the numerous population, not to mention the many fish, game, all sorts of poultry, and especially the marvelously large lobsters, whose claws are each as large as a man's hand.

Turtles I often saw of a size that it took a man to carry one. A hen costs 6 kreuzers, and eggs are sometimes to be had 20 for a batzen (4 kr.). A turkey is worth 24 to 30 kr. A bushel of rye, 2 shillings, or 36 kr. A bushel of good wheat, 3 shillings or 54 kr. Fruit sells well; it is mostly taken across the sea to other countries. But all other goods cost twice or three times as much as in Germany, because they have to be taken all the way there; therefore, what can be bought for a florin in Germany, costs 4 or 5 fl. in Pennsylvania and the neighboring countries. Domestic linen, which costs from 15 to 18 kreuzers in Germany, brings 40 kr. or even a florin in these English colonies. A pair of man's shoes costs 2 to 3 florins, and even more; a pair of stockings quite as much.

Of beverages there are many kinds in Pennsylvania and the other English colonies; in the first place, delicious and healthy water; secondly, they make a mixture of milk and three parts water; thirdly, good apple cider; fourthly, small beer; fifthly, delicious English strong, sweet

sweet beer; sixthly, punch, which consists of three parts water and one part West India rum (when no rum is to be had, brandy is taken, but rum is much pleasanter), mixed with sugar and lemon juice; seventhly, sinkere [sangaree], which is still more delicious to drink; this is made of two parts water and one part Spanish wine with sugar and nutmeg; and eighthly, German and Spanish wines, to be had plentifully at all taverns; of the latter, a quart costs a rix-dollar. Mixed drinks are all drunk from china vessels, which are called poole [bowls], and are formed like a soup-dish.

All trades and professions have good earnings; beggars are nowhere to be seen, for each county or township cares and provides for its poor. In the country the people live so far from one another that many a one has to walk fifteen minutes or half an hour to get to his nearest neighbor. The reason is because many a farmer has 50 or 100 and even 200—400 acres of land, laid out in orchards, meadows, fields and woods. Such a one has usually 10, 15 or 20 acres in orchards alone, from which a great deal of cider and brandy is made.

Peach and cherry trees many a farmer plants in whole avenues from one plantation to the other, and they yield an abundant crop. One sort of peaches are inside and outside red, as large

large as a lemon, but round and smooth, and they are ripe about St. Bartholomew's day. Again there are some waxen yellow, red streaked, and green as grass. There is also a sort called clingstones; they are sweet when they are ripe; they are often preserved before they are quite ripe, like cucumbers. Pears there are but few, and damsons none, because they will not thrive and are often spoiled by the mildew.

Every farmer pastures his cattle, horses and sheep on his own farm, or lets them run about in the bushes, and brings them home in the evening and morning to have the cows milked, and then lets them run at large again all night till morning; so that the animals find their own food and need not be fed daily as in Germany. No cattle are stabled during the summer, except when a cow is to calve; but frequently one seeks and finds the old and the young together in the forest, or a cow comes unexpectedly home with her calf. Throughout the whole province no shepherd or cowherd is needed, because all cattle and sheep are kept in fenced fields or let run at large in the fields, where they find plenty of food and moreover spoil much in many places.

In the rural districts of Pennsylvania the newborn children are not brought to church to receive

ceive the holy baptism till they are a fortnight, several weeks, three or six months, and sometimes a whole year old; so that such large and wild children often kick at the preacher or baptist, thus giving rise to laughter. Many Pennsylvanian mothers are in the habit of suckling their unruly babies in church, even during the holy baptism. Many parents act as sponsors for their own children, because they have no faith or confidence in other people in this important point; for which they are not to be blamed, for many a one will not say what he believes. Others, although baptized themselves, will not permit their children to be baptized. When questioned about it they answer they can see no difference between the baptized and the unbaptized young people; that no one keeps his baptismal vows, and that it is not necessary, therefore, to pay the minister a dollar for it. In my school in Pennsylvania I had many adult persons of either sex who, in answer to my question if they had been baptized, said: No, what's the use of it? Whereupon I endeavored to shake their unbelief by quoting Nicodemus' conversation with Jesus, and thus I brought many young people to a recognition of the necessity of the holy baptism, so that they became quite anxious and desired to be baptized. Some were also eager to learn
the

the principal points of the whole Evangelical Christian doctrine, which many parents would not permit, saying that they did not send their children to school to learn a faith, but to learn to read and write as much as was necessary.

In Pennsylvania, as throughout North America, from Acadia to Mexico, plenty of wild black and white vines may be seen, which grow in the forests around the oak-trees and along the hedges. Many a vine is at the bottom as thick as a tree, and it often is so full of grapes that the boughs of the trees bend beneath them. In the blossom time the grapes have a very strong odor, and in October they are ripe. They make some wine of them, but it costs much sugar. Large quantities of grapes are taken to the market of Philadelphia. Such grapes would be much better if the vines were cut as in Europe; but as the people live too far apart, and as the wild animals and birds would do much injury to the vines, there will be no vine growing for a long time to come.

Sassafras trees, which are not to be found in Europe, are plentiful here; the best breast-tea can be made of its blossoms; the wood and the roots are especially good for medicines. There are trees that are as thick as a man around the loins. The leaves look and smell like laurel leaves; the blossoms are gold-colored, just like the

the primrose, but much finer. For my home-journey, I collected and took with me a package of sassafras flowers or blossoms, which were my best medicine on my voyage.

There are many sugar-trees* here which are as thick and high as an oak-tree; in spring, when they are in full sap, the sugar-water may be tapped from them. I tried it myself, and in March when they begin to flow, I bored a hole at the bottom of the tree through the bark and inserted a small tube made of a quill, through which the sugar-water flowed, just as one clarifies brandy. In fifteen minutes I had a small tumbler full of sugar-water. The people who gather such sugar-water, fill a kettle with it and let it boil till it is thick, and when it has become cold it is a thick honey. The sugar-trees usually stand in forests near the brooks, and they grow wild.

The beautiful tulip-trees† grow frequently there. In the month of May, when they are in blossoms, they are full of tulips; these look yellow and tabbied red, and are as natural as

---

* This species of trees is described under the name of maple-trees in the History of the French Colonies of North America, p. 213. M. De Diereville calls them wild fig-trees.

† These tulip-trees are known to the French in Louisiana under the name of *tulipier* as a sort of laurel-trees. See the above quoted book, p. 334.

those

those that grow out of the ground [from bulbs].
The trees are as thick and high as the tallest
cherry-trees. I saw another species of tulip-
trees with their blossoms, which are planted in
the gardens, but are not larger than dwarf apple
or pear trees; they do not bloom until August,
and are white and tabbied red. Of the first-
named larger species of tulip-trees no blossoms
are seen until they are 20 years old and over.
Many other kinds and species of trees, flowers
and herbs, and also grain are found in America.
The daisy, for instance, which is so frequent and
therefore so little esteemed with us, is as rare
in Pennsylvania as the rarest and most beautiful
flowers in Europe can be, for it is planted in the
gardens as a rare flower. Quite as rare there,
is the juniper-shrub, which is esteemed much
higher than the rosemary with us, and the
juniper-berries are sold for a higher price than
peppercorns. The juniper-shrubs are also cultivated in gardens. Quite as rare are all other
European flowers and herbs. And so, what is
not highly esteemed in Germany is rare and
dear in America; and vice-versa, what is not
highly esteemed here is precious in Germany.
The Germans who have emigrated to America
miss many good things there, the Würtembergers and Rhinelanders especially the generous
juice of the grape.

All

All through Pennsylvania not a single meadow-saffron is seen in the gardens and meadows in autumn.

The wood in the above-named new country grows fast and is much taller, but less durable than with us. It is quite surprising how dense the forests are, and what beautiful, smooth, thick and tall trees they contain. There are many kinds of trees, mostly oaks, but they are not so fruitful as those in Germany. After these there are also beech-trees, but not many. Birch-trees are rarely found, but I saw some that were very tall and as thick as a thick oak-tree. I have already spoken of the poplars; they have soft wood which looks snow-white inside; there are many of them. Walnut-trees are exceedingly plentiful; this beautiful coffee-brown and hard wood is precious and useful, because all sorts of fine and elegant household furniture are made of it. When cut, a great deal of it is shipped to Holland, England, Ireland and other countries where it brings a high price. These walnut-trees bear every year nuts which are as large as a medium-sized apple, from which much oil is made. They have bark and leaves like our large nut-trees. Our large German walnut-trees are little cultivated as yet. There are but few hazel-nut shrubs in the forests, but of chestnut-trees there is a multitude;

tude; no less so of Hecker (hickory) nuts which are larger than hazel-nuts, but are held in little esteem. Indian or wild-cherry trees are not seen very frequently; I myself broke such Indian cherries from the trees and ate them, but they are not so good as European cherries. In the Pennsylvania forests one finds no thorn or sloe hedges, no downy gooseberries and the like. The greatest ornament of the forests are the beautiful and excellent cedar-trees; they grow mostly in the high mountains. This wood has a very strong odor, is as light as foam, and especially precious for organ-pipes; for the pipes made of said cedar-wood have a much finer and purer tone than those of tin, of which I have seen sufficient proofs. All houses in Philadelphia are roofed with shingles of cedar-wood. When a heavy rain pours down upon it, this wood sounds like a roof of copper or brass.

No May-bugs or cock-chafers are seen in this country in spring; but every fifth year it has a terrible plague of vermin called *Lockis* [locusts],* which are somewhat larger than the May-bugs and can do immense injury to fields and forests. Red and white snails are not found here, and the frogs have a very different voice. They do

---

* This creature seems to be a species of grasshoppers. Perhaps the word *Lockis* is derived from *Locusta*.

not

not croak or quack, but yelp. And this yelping begins as early as March.

In America there are quite different kinds of birds to be seen from those in Europe. Of birds which are precisely like our European ones, no others are found but ravens, swallows, and the little hedge-sparrows. The American birds are most beautiful; their splendid colors and lovely song are above all praise. In the first place there are birds which are yellow and have black wings; secondly, red ones with black wings; thirdly, altogether yellow ones; fourthly, starlings which are larger than ours, look quite blue and have red wings; fifthly, brilliant red ones with plumes on their head; sixthly, entirely blue ones; seventhly, white ones with black wings; eighthly, many-colored ones; ninthly, grass-green ones with red heads; tenthly, there is a species which is black, white and pied. These birds can imitate the singing and whistling of all birds; in half an hour such a bird can imitate more than 30 birds successfully. There is a species of birds that call in summer all day long quite plainly: "Get you gone! Get you gone!" Another, which is heard mostly by night, calls: "Wipperwill! Wipperwill!" [Whip-poor-Will]; it is called by that name. We find in Pennsylvania no storks, no magpie, no cuckoo, no lark, no yellow-hammer, no nightingale, no quail,

quail, no thistle-bird or gold-finch, no canary-bird, no black-bird, no tom-tit, no robin-red-breast, no red-wing, and no sparrow. It may be that some of the Pennsylvania birds resemble the above-named somewhat, but they are not altogether like them; there is a difference either in size, or in color, or in the song, or in something else. Thus we might consider the bird that calls out his "Get you gone!" in almost the same measure in which our quails call, as a quail; but it has a small tail, such as our quails do not have.

The most wonderful bird, not only in Pennsylvania, but perhaps in the whole world, is a small bird which is rarely seen. This little bird is not quite so large as a May-bug, but only as large as a gold-bird. It glitters like gold, and sometimes it appears green, blue and red. Its beak is rather long, and as sharp as a needle; its feet are like fine wire. It sips only the honey from the flowers; hence it has the name of sugar-bird.* It builds its nest in the flowers

---

* Father Charlevoix describes it under the name of fly-bird, and shows that it is even handsomer than the humming-bird. See the History and Trade of the French Colonies of North America, published by Mezler, p. 248. But we will hear another author with respect to this rare bird. This is M. De Diereville, in his Journey to Acadia, which is found in the Collection of Journeys, published in Göttingen.

flowers in a garden; the nest is not larger than a cupping-glass, but there are generally 4 or 5 young ones in it. It moves its wings with indescribable swiftness, making a loud hissing with

---

Göttingen. From his work, p. 237, we quote the following: We shall now speak of little birds whose eggs have no such depredations to fear, because they are no larger than hempseed; these are the eggs of the humming-birds or fly-birds, which are the finest in the world, and whose colors are so lively that it seems as if they emitted fiery sparks beneath their throats, especially the males. It is impossible to imagine anything more varied and at the same time more brilliant than these colors. But these birds are only seen at the time of the year when there are flowers, for they fly like bees from one to the other, in order to sip the sweet juice from the pale as well as the reddish ones. All these various movements they perform with the utmost swiftness; no other bird equals them in this respect, and they can scarcely be seen when they whir through the air. The same nimbleness they show in all that they do. They do not, for instance, settle upon the flowers in order to suck the sweet honey-juice concealed in their delicate tubes; but they only flap their wings incessantly and with such swiftness around the flower that it is impossible to describe it. The way how nature, the wise moulder, has formed the beak and tongue of these little birds is really admirable. Their black and thin, pointed and almost perfectly straight beak is about a finger's breadth in length; their delicate split tongue is twice as long. Inserting the latter into a flower and moving it constantly, they fill it with the sweetness contained in every flower.

By

with them. When it does not fly, one can hear it sing very softly and gracefully when one is fortunate enough to get quite near it. I

By means of a natural force peculiar to the tongue this juice is subsequently led into their little stomachs, and it constitutes their sole food. They have a light gray belly, a silver-green back, and a black tail with white spots; their black wings and legs fit their little bodies perfectly; the body is no thicker than the point of a child's finger. And in The Account of Nova Scotia, 8mo, Frankfort, 1750, p. 174 f., this bird is described as follows: Among all birds that occur here the most curious is the *murmur* (hummer, humming-bird), of which there are two species. The one is exceedingly small, with all its feathers not larger than a small fly. The other makes a big noise in the ears like the humming of a large fly, which is not much larger. Its claws, which are of the length of a thumb's breadth, seem to be fine needles, and so also its beak, which is merely the case of another beak which it puts out and sticks into the middle of the flowers, in order to extract the honey which is its food. In short, this creature is worthy to be called an ornament of nature. This bird wears a black plume on its crest which is of extraordinary beauty; its breast resembles the most beautiful rose-color one can see, and its belly is as white as milk. Its back, wings and tail are of the finest gray color that resembles a rose, and shaded all around with a brilliant gold color. Its down, which can hardly be seen, and which covers its whole plumage, is wavelike, which gives it so delicate an appearance that it resembles a flower; all this is so delicate and pretty that it is impossible to describe it.

will

will not say for how much money this little bird is sometimes bought by great people. But they do not live long, as it is impossible to furnish them with their proper food.

In Pennsylvania multitudes of fish can be caught every spring in the Delaware and Schuylkill rivers, and lots of wild pigeons can be shot twice a year, viz., in spring when they migrate to the north, and in fall when they come back and migrate to the south. The fish ascend at their season from the sea, and what are not caught go about the end of May back into the sea. These fish are an ell long and almost half an ell broad; so many are often caught that many a one salts a whole barrel or tub full of them, enough for a year; when one wants to eat some, they are laid in fresh water over night, then washed and fried. In the same manner the pigeons, too, are salted and eaten in winter.*

There is not so much game and wild-fowl around Philadelphia as there formerly was, because that region is thickly inhabited, and because every one may shoot what he will. But the farther one gets into the country the less it is inhabited, and the more one finds of all kinds of game, especially much feathered game, and

---

* With respect to these pigeons, see above quoted book, p. 306.

many a one supports himself in this country by hunting.

In Pennsylvania one finds in summer time many species of snakes and other vermin, especially in the Blue Mountains. Many a snake, 10, 12, 15, and even 18 feet long has been seen there, and many persons and animals have been mortally bitten by these terrible and dangerous creatures. There are black and white, green and gray snakes, also black ones with yellow stripes. Among these the rattlesnakes are the largest and worst; but in some respects the black snakes, which are 12 to 15 feet long, and as thick as an arm, are even more dangerous, inasmuch as they have a marvelous power to charm, and that only by their steady glance; so that every creature, be it a hare, a bird or a squirrel, must come down from the trees and close up to them, when they pounce upon it and devour it.* They can climb the tallest oaks and other trees, and they are also able to charm little children, so that they must stand still before them. The children cry pite-

---

* This account sounds rather strange, and I should be inclined to regard it as a fable palmed off upon the author if I had not read the same in the Description of Nova Scotia, above alluded to, pp. 213, 214. But here the power of fascinating is ascribed to the rattle-snakes, while our author attributes it to the black snakes.

ously,

ously, and it has often happened that they were saved, and that large snakes were found lying before them. The rattle-snakes are in part even larger than the above-mentioned species; many of them are more than 18 feet long and as thick as a hay pole. These snakes have at their rear end rattle-tails with which they can rattle so that it can be heard from afar. They rattle whenever they are angry or see anybody. They add every year a new ring to their rattle-tails. These snakes have scales like the fish; the scales are black, blue and green, and look like mother-of-pearl. Snakes have frequently crept into the houses and even into the beds of people who live in the woods, so that the people lay on them in the night till the snakes grow restless beneath the weight, whereupon they are driven out and killed.

One of the beauties of Pennsylvania are the fire-flies that fly about so plentifully by night in the summer time, that it seems as if it were snowing fire. Some years ago a newly arrived German man was badly scared by them; for as he was working in the field late one evening, and some fire-flies, which were totally unknown to him, were flying about him, our honest Hans was so frightened that he dropped everything and ran hastily home. As he came in fear and trembling to his family, he said: "O God, shield and

and protect us! How many fiery spirits fly about in this country! O God, would I were in Germany again!"

The Blue Mountains lie in Pennsylvania, about thirty hours' journey from Philadelphia. This mountain range begins at the Delaware River, and passes to the left across the country, and reaches as far as the great river Ohio. It is very high, and it can therefore be seen already in the Delaware Bay before we get to Philadelphia. These Blue Mountains extend over 40 hours' journey.

Of the savages, or Indians, who hold intercourse with the English, there is a great multitude; they live even beyond the Ohio, and the Hudson River on which Albany lies; therefore on both sides to the right and left of Pennsylvania. These two waters, which are very large, are about 100 hours' journey from Philadelphia. These savages live in the bush in huts, away from said waters, and so far inland that no one is able to find the end of the habitations of these savages. The farther we get into the country, the more savages we see. They support themselves in various ways; some shoot game, others dig roots, some raise tobacco and Indian corn or maize, which they eat raw or boiled; besides, they deal also in all sorts of hides, in beaver-skins and costly furs.

The

The savages that live on the borders of the Europeans are frequently seen; some of them understand a little English. I myself have several times seen whole families; once I had occasion, at the request of Captain Von Diemer, to play the organ to a savage family, when they became very gay and manifested their surprise and joy by signs and genuflections. These Indians, who walk about amid other people, wear instead of clothes, blankets, such as are usually used as covers for the horses; these they have hanging uncut and unsewed about their bare bodies. They wear no coverings on their heads or on their feet. The form of their bodies does not differ from ours, except that they look dark yellow, which, however, is not their natural color, for they besmear and stain themselves thus; but at their birth they are born as white as we are. Both men and women have long, smooth hair on their heads; the men do not tolerate beards; and when in their youth, the hairs begin to grow, they pull them out immediately; they have, therefore, smooth faces like the women. On account of the lacking beard and the sameness in dressing, it is not easy to distinguish the men from the women. When these savages wish to be good-looking, they paint their cheeks and foreheads red, hang their ears with strings of false beads of an ell's length. They wear neither shirts, nor breeches, nor coats beneath their blankets. In their wilderness where they live the young and old go about naked in the summer time. Every autumn they come in large crowds to the city of Philadelphia, bringing with them all sorts of little baskets which they make quite neatly and beautifully, many skins and costly furs. Besides these things they trade off to the Governor, when they are assembled, a tract of land of more than a thousand acres, which is yet all forest. In the name of the country and the city they are annually presented with many things, such as blankets, guns, rum or brandy and the like; on which occasion they make merry with their own strange Indian songs, especially when they are drunk. No one understands their language; some of them who come much in contact with the English, can speak a little English. There are very strong, tall and courageous people among them. In their language they *thou* and *thee* everybody, even the Governor, and they can run as fast as the deer. When you speak to them of the true and everlasting God, the Creator of heaven and earth, they do not understand it, but answer simply: They believe that there are two men, a good one and a bad one; that the good one had made everything

thing good, and the bad one had made everything bad; that it was not necessary, therefore, to pray to the good one, as he was doing no one any harm; but the bad one should be prayed to that he might do no one any harm. Of a resurrection of the dead, a salvation, heaven or hell, they know and understand nothing. They bury their dead where they die. I have often been told by truthful people that very old savages that can hardly move any longer, or break down on the way, are simply killed and buried. But if a savage kills another, unless it be in war or on account of old age, whether the murdered was one of our or one of their own people, the murderer must surely die. They take him first to their Indian King to be tried, and thence to the place where the murder was committed, slay him suddenly, bury him on the spot, and cover his grave with much wood and stones. On the other hand, they must likewise be given satisfaction in similar cases, otherwise they would treat an innocent person of our people in like manner.

When the savages come to the city of Philadelphia and see the handsome and magnificent buildings there, they wonder and laugh at the Europeans for expending so much toil and cost on houses. They say that it is quite unnecessary,

sary, as one can live without such houses. Still more they wonder at the garments of the Europeans and their costly finery; they will even spit out when they see it.

When a savage couple are betrothed, the man gives his affianced bride a piece of a deer's leg into her hand, whereby he gives to understand that he will nourish his future wife with meat; his affianced, on the other hand, gives him an ear of corn, in token that she will provide her future husband and children with bread. Thus they care for each other, and remain together until death parts them.

Old savages have often been questioned about their descent and origin, and they have answered that all they knew or could say was this; that their great-grandparents had lived in these same wildernesses, and that it was not right that the Europeans came and took their lands away from them. For this reason they must move farther and farther back in the wilderness to find game for their food.

The weapon with which these savages shoot is a round bow, in the front centre of which they place a sharp and pointed stone of a finger's length; in the rear it is rather more than an inch wide, and on both sides as sharp as a knife; they aim accurately with it, and when they have wounded a deer which will not fall they run after

after it till they get it, for they can run faster than a horse. In witness of this I have brought such a stone home with me wherewith the Indians, or savages, have shot game. This was their only shooting weapon before they obtained guns from the Europeans.

There is something remarkable that was discovered by Rev. Mr. SCHÄRTEL or SCHÄRTLIN, who was a minister in Zell and Altbach in the Duchy of Wurtemberg, but who now serves as a preacher in Pennsylvania, in the township of Magunsche [Macungy] in the Blue Mountains. Some 60 miles from Philadelphia, A. D. 1753, when he had gone astray and was seeking the right way, he chanced to find in the wilderness, in a small wooded hill, a stone door frame which stuck in the ground. At first he thought it was a work of nature; but when he had rubbed off the moss with which it was overgrown, and when he regarded it attentively, he found in the upper stone a legend chiseled out in Hebrew, in the following words: THUS FAR THE GOD OF JOSHUA HAS HELPED US.

But although so many foundations for building houses have been laid here and there throughout this new country, and although so large tracts of woods and fields have been cleared far and wide, nowhere, except beside a small creek near Philadelphia, have traces of old

old habitations been found, such as hewn stones laid one upon the other, from which it could have been surmised that some building must have been standing on the spot before the time of the savages.

In Pennsylvania everything is paid for with stamped paper money, for which one can have and buy whatever one wishes. Said paper money is printed in the English language, and with the King's coat-of-arms and the Governor's name. The smallest piece makes 3 kr.,* the 2d 4 kr., the 3d 6 kr., the 4th 9 kr., the 5th 15 kr., the 6th 20 kr., the 7th 30 kr., the 8th is half a crown which makes 42 kr., the 9th is a whole crown which makes as much again, and the 10th is a twenty-shilling bill which is one pound, or 6 florins German money. Such a piece of paper money is not larger than a hand's breadth; on it stand in part 6, 12, 18 or 24 florins; such paper money can be ex-

---

* The author has here taken a *kreuzer* for a *pence* (penny).

TRANSLATOR'S NOTE.—The German annotator is wrong. The author did not take a German *kreuzer* for an English *penny;* he simply reduced the English money to the value of German money. The original reads: "Das kleinste Stück thut 3 kr.," i. e. *does*, or *makes*, or *is equivalent to* 3 kr. The author makes his meaning very clear in: "das 8te ist eine halbe Crone, welches thut 42 kr." (—which makes 42 kr.)

changed

changed for silver and gold. If any one counterfeits or prints such stamped paper money, he is hanged without pardon. Beside the paper money there is no other currency but gold, French and Spanish dollars, the last named having a large circulation.

N. B. If our countrymen bring German coin to that country, they will not get a kreuzer's worth for such money: that is, if it be small coin.

When two persons have a quarrel or lawsuit in this country, and if they cannot settle it themselves, they must first appear before a Justice, who is as much as a judge. When the plaintiff and his witnesses prefer a charge, the Justice asks if they can swear to it. When the question is answered in the affirmative, the Justice takes the Bible into his hand and admonishes the parties once more very sharply. When this is done, one must take the Bible out of the Justice's hand and kiss it three times. The Justice says: Now it is done. He sits down again and binds the defendant over for the next court, and sends him immediately by the constable, that is the court officer, to the prison in Philadelphia, where he must stay till the next court is held, which is sometimes almost a quarter of a year. But if the defendant will not go to prison, he must usually bind himself

himself in the sum of from 100 to 600 florins to appear and surrender himself at the next court at Philadelphia. But if he cannot do that, he must look about for some good friend to bind himself for him. If he does not appear at the appointed time, the deposited money, or property to the same amount, is irredeemably forfeited. When a case comes for the first time before the court, it costs already 5 pounds, that is 30 florins; if it is not disposed of, but postponed to the second court, it costs as much again, and yet the case is not always disposed of then; but the gentlemen of the court choose, when it has been called up often enough, three impartial men who are to dispose of it. This is done in the following manner: When the three selected men meet at the appointed time with the plaintiff and the defendant, two of the referees are told for which party each had been chosen and sworn by the court; but the third man, being the arbitrator, must decide when the two cannot agree. But before the case itself is taken up, an English bill of complaint is made out by the three men in the presence of an English clerk, even if German people are concerned in the case, for a German document is of no validity before the authorities. Both the plaintiff and the defendant must sign this document and promise that both parties will abide

abide by that which the three men will do, conclude and decide in the matter. Then the case is taken up to be adjudged in favor of the one or the other party.

If any one contracts debts, and does not or cannot pay them at the appointed time, the best that he has is taken away from him; but if he has nothing, or not enough, he must go immediately to prison and remain there till some one vouches for him, or till he is sold. This is done whether he has children or not. But if he wishes to be released and has children, such a one is frequently compelled to sell a child. If such a debtor owes only 5 pounds, or 30 florins, he must serve for it a year or longer, and so in proportion to his debt; but if a child of 8, 10 or 12 years of age is given for it, said child must serve until he or she is 21 years old.

If a man in Pennsylvania is betrothed to a woman, and does not care to be married by an ordained preacher, he may be married by any Justice, wherever he will, without having the banns published, on payment of 6 florins. It is a very common custom among the newly married, when the priest has blessed them, to kiss each other in presence of the whole church assemblage, or wherever the marriage ceremony takes place. Again, when a couple have been published from the pulpit, even if this has been done

done for the second or third time, they are still at liberty to give each other up without the least cost. Even when such a couple have come to the church with their wedding guests, nay, when they already stand before the altar, and one party repents the engagement, he or she may yet walk away. This has frequently been done; but it occurs oftener that a bride leaves her bridegroom together with the wedding guests in the church, which causes a cruel laughter among said wedding guests; these may then freely partake of the meal that has been prepared.

If a couple in this province want to marry each other, and the parents and relatives on one or both sides will not permit it, especially when a woman will not renounce her lover, they ride off and away together on one horse. And because women have greater privileges than men, the man must sit on the horse behind his beloved. In this position they ride to a Justice, and say they had stolen each other, and request him to marry them for their money. When this is done, no one, neither parents nor friends, can afterward separate them.

If any one has lost a wife or husband in Germany, and if such loss was not caused by the death of either of them, he or she can find such lost treasure, if the same be still alive, in America,

America, for Pennsylvania is the gathering place of all runaways and good-for-nothings. Many women and men are there who have deserted their spouses and their children, and have married again, but in doing so have generally made a worse bargain than before.

If a man gets a woman with child, and he marries her, either before or after her confinement, he has expiated his guilt and is not punished by the authorities. But if he will not marry the woman whom he got with child, and she sues him, he must either marry her, or give her a sum of money. But there is no penalty on fornication.

A few years ago the following incident truly happened not far from the Blue Mountains. A man's wife, who was well advanced in years, fell sick and grew worse from day to day. When the woman had given up all hope of recovery, she commended herself to God and begged her husband not to refuse her last request, which would be for his own and her children's benefit. Her husband declared his readiness to comply with her wish so far as he would be able to do so, gave her his hand, and asked her to name her request. She said: Alas, my dear husband, I am much concerned about my children, who are young and not grown up yet; and I fear that

that when I die they may get a bad stepmother; I pray you earnestly, therefore, to marry no other than our Rosina, who has all this time been a faithful and industrious servant in our house. But her husband comforted her, saying that she should set her mind at rest, that he hoped she would recover from her illness. This she would not believe, and she persisted in urging her husband that he would marry no other than Rosina, so that she might know and see before her end what sort of a mother her children would have. Her husband had, therefore, to promise the suggested marriage with mouth and hand. But this did not yet satisfy her; she also sent for Rosina to come to her bedside, and commended her household, together with her husband and children, to her care. The servant maid did not say nay, but submitted everything to her master's will. When the anxious woman had received the promise of both, her husband and the servant had to join hands before her eyes, vowing that they would keep each other. The sick woman then laid her hands upon theirs and blessed this new couple herself, and was very glad of it. But after this the sick woman grew better from day to day, and at last perfectly well. The husband then said to his old wife: You have yourself given me this young woman for a wife; now I will keep

keep her as such. Whereupon his old wife said: Yes, I will have it so, in order that I may die in peace whenever my time comes. The young wife gave birth to children during the lifetime of the old one, and the old one tended and nursed the young one always well and faithfully during her confinements; so that these two wives and their husband were very well pleased with each other. And no one interfered, because they were separatists and not churchpeople. Whenever any one came, wishing to speak to the mistress of the house, the husband or one of his wives would always ask which one was meant, the old one or the young one? And they admitted it themselves that they were both his wives.

In order to impugn the credibility of this story some may remind me of the severity of the English law which unmercifully dooms to death him who has two wives, or her who has two husbands. But the judge does not pronounce this doom if the other party does not bring suit. These two wives were satisfied, and there was in this case the special circumstance that severe as the laws are, they cannot be executed so strictly in Pennsylvania, because the people in the rural parts live too widely separated from each other. If it should really happen that a man had two wives, and the case should be brought

brought to the notice of the courts, he would not rest till he had married a third wife. Then he would be free, and would not have sinned against the law which merely prohibits the marrying of two wives, but does not expressly prohibit the marrying of three wives.

On the whole, crimes are punished severely, especially larceny. If any one steals only a handkerchief, a pair of stockings or shoes, or a shirt, or the like things of little value, and suit is brought against him, he is tied to a post in the public market, stripped to the waist, and so terribly lashed with a switch, or a horse- or dog-whip, to which knots are sometimes attached, that patches of skin and flesh hang down from his body. But if such a culprit should subsequently steal again, and were it only an object worth 20 florins, or a horse, short work is made with him. They place him in a cart, drive him beneath the gallows, throw a rope round his neck, hang him up, drive the cart away beneath him, and let him dangle; sometimes the culprit suffers long and dies miserably. For in this country it does not matter who plays the hangman; for 5 pounds or 30 florins any one will do it. During the time while I was there such an execution took place, when an unskilled hangman had to hang a thief, which took him so long that some distinguished gentlemen, who

who were present, grew impatient and called out to him to know why he was fooling around so long with him. But the hangman was quick-witted and answered boldly: If you, gentlemen, can hang a man better than I can, just come on. The consequence was that the gentlemen were laughed at by the people.

Every one here is at liberty to take his fallen horse, cow, or other animal out wherever he chooses, dispensing with the services of a flayer, to take the skin off the dead animal, and to do with it as he pleases. No obstacle is placed in his way herein, and it may be practised by any one, whatever his business or profession may be, without encountering any remonstrance.

In Pennsylvania one might travel about a whole year without spending a penny; for it is customary in this country that, when one comes with his horse to a house, the traveler is asked if he wishes to have something to eat, whereupon the stranger is served with a piece of cold meat which has been left over from dinner; in addition to this he is provided with fine bread, butter and cheese, also with plenty to drink. If one wishes to stay over night, he and his horse are harbored free of charge. If any one comes to a house at meal-time, he is asked to take his seat at the table and to take pot-luck. But there

there are also taverns where everything may be had.

English women in Pennsylvania and in all the English colonies have all the qualities and privileges of women in old England. They are exceedingly handsome and well formed, generally gay, friendly, very free, plucky, smart and clever, but also very haughty, they are fond of dress and demand great attention from the men. The English men make much of them and show them great respect. A man must not think of marrying a woman unless he is able to support her without expecting work of her; otherwise she would make him unhappy, or even desert him; for they must not be asked to do any household work except such as they will do of their own free choice. They are fond of receiving visits and attending parties; whether the husband likes it or not, he must not even show a dissatisfied mien. I would rather beat three men in England than box a woman's ear but slightly; and if such a thing is done by her own husband and she complains to her neighbors, his life is not safe. But if such a thing happens repeatedly, he had better put a safe distance between himself and her, as she can send him to prison, if not to a galley, for a long time. No one can compel her to receive her husband again. That English women are generally very handsome

handsome is not surprising, for they are tenderly nurtured from their childhood; they eat and drink no coarse food and beverages: they need not work and are not much exposed to the sun. In court the evidence of one woman is worth as much as that of three male witnesses. It is said they received this great privilege from Queen Elizabeth.

Respecting the extent of America, they say in Pennsylvania that that continent is much larger than Europe, but that it is impossible to explore it on account of its immeasurable pathless forests and its great and small rivers. Nor is Pennsylvania an island, as some simpletons in Germany believe it to be. I have had occasion to speak of the extent of this continent with an English traveler who had been far in the interior of the country among the savages. He told me that he had been more than 700 English miles, which is 233 Swabian hours' journey from Philadelphia, purchasing skins and all sorts of furs from the savages. He had spoken on that very same topic with an Indian, a very old fellow, who had given him to understand in English that he and his brothers had one time journeyed from the place, where the meeting with said English traveler had occurred, straight through the land and through the bush toward the setting sun, and that according to their estimate

estimate they had gone 1600 English miles. But seeing that there was no hope of finding the end of this country they had returned. On this journey they had met an indescribable multitude of Indians of their race, also all sorts of animals, as, white and black bears, stags that are not so large as ours, wild oxen [buffaloes], panthers that are strong enough to kill cattle or men, wild hogs that are very large, wolves, monkeys, foxes and the like. Besides feathered creatures of many kinds, as, golden eagles, torckis [turkeys], *i. e.* a kind of fowl that are larger than roosters; swans, wild ducks, not to mention the many strange kinds of birds that they, the savages, had not known before, and many animals covered with very fine and costly fur. They had also met an animal which had a smooth and pointed horn an ell and a half long on its head; said horn pointed straight ahead. This animal was as large as a middle-sized horse, but swifter than a stag in running. The Europeans of Philadelphia had taken this animal for the unicorn.* The old savage also said they had met on this journey many great waters, besides smaller rivers, all of which they had crossed by swimming.

In the Blue Mountains various rich ores have been found which are kept concealed as yet as

---

* Perhaps it is the Elk.

much

much as possible; this ore consists for the most part in copper, sulphur and iron, and promises a rich yield.

Iron-works and foundries and glass-works have already been established. Much cast-iron and glass are exported from this province in ships sailing to Ireland, England, Holland, and to the other colonies; many a ship leaves the port of Philadelphia, freighted exclusively with iron bars.

A place has also been found in Pennsylvania, which is very well known to me, where the most beautiful blue, white and red marble may be had of which the English build very fine altars, halls and columns. These stones are as large as one would have them; there are also plenty of other fine stones for building purposes. Freestone and unhewn blocks are, therefore, almost exclusively used for building in this country.

In Pennsylvania there are already four printing offices, two of which are in Philadelphia, one in the English and the other in the German language; the third is in Germantown and the fourth in Lancaster.

There are also various flour-mills, saw-mills, oil-presses, fulling-mills, powder-mills and paper-mills, lime and brick-kilns, and not a few tanneries and potteries. In Philadelphia there are also

also German and English apothecaries, and I know of no art or trade that is not to be found in that city and in that new land. Even glaziers and scissors-grinders are already going around, which appears very strange and ridiculous to the English people.

Nothing is lacking in this country except, as I have stated before, the cultivation of the vine, but I have no doubt that this, too, will come in time. It is no wonder, therefore, that this beautiful country, which is already extensively settled and inhabited by rich people, has excited the covetousness of France. And actually, while I write this, it is rumored that the French had made a raid into Pennsylvania in November, 1755, and had taken Lancaster, a surprise rendered easy by the dissensions between the Governor, Mr. Morris, and the Assembly, which latter had refused to vote money for the defense of the country. But according to my humble opinion, Pennsylvania cannot stand a long war; there is nothing for which it is less prepared than a war, especially because so many Quakers are there who will not quarrel or fight with anybody. For this reason no magazines or stores have ever been established and filled with grain and provisions. Hitherto every one has sent his annual surplus products to Philadelphia to be sold there, and from there they are shipped by sea to other provinces;

provinces; I believe, therefore, that for want of provisions in this war time there must soon arise an indescribable dearth.

Compared to Europe, Pennsylvania has a very changeable climate; in summer it is often so hot and almost without a breeze that one is near suffocating; and in winter intensely cold spells are quite frequent and come so suddenly that men and beasts, and even the birds in the air are in danger of freezing to death. Fortunately these cold spells are of short duration and are interrupted by a sudden change. There are often in one day three or four kinds of weather: warm, cold, storm and wind, rain or snow, and then fine weather again. Sometimes cyclonic winds and cloudbursts come so suddenly and unexpectedly that it seems as if everything was doomed to destruction. Large fruit and cedar trees are occasionally torn out of the ground together with their roots; now and then even whole tracts of forests are blown down. There are constantly many violent winds in this country, because it is so near the open sea.

In spring the warm weather comes so suddenly that everything grows very fast, and in the beginning of June harvesting has fully begun.

In summer time, no matter how hot it may have been during the day, no one must remain lightly clad in the evening after sunset, on account

count of the sharp and heavy dew; those who neglect this precaution are sure to have a catarrh or a fever.

It is surprising to hear old Indians or savages complain and say that, since the Europeans came into their country, they were so frequently visited by heavy snow-falls, severe frosts, and torrents of rain, of which they had known nothing before the coming of the Europeans. Whether this is true or not, even the Pennsylvanians ascribe the facts to the Europeans, because these, and especially the Germans, are mostly such fearful swearers.

For this reason a penalty of 5 pounds or 30 florins has recently been fixed throughout Pennsylvania upon every oath uttered in public, in order to check this shocking habit of swearing, both among the English and the Germans. If any one hears another swear, and informs against him, such informer is to have one-half of the imposed fine, or 15 florins; the consequence being that many a one is trying hard to guard against being caught in the act of swearing. On the other hand, many a one has been induced by this law to turn informer for the purpose of earning money. During my sojourn in the country one of these greedy informers got something which he had not bargained for. Having from interested motives informed against

against a very poor man for swearing, the Justice asked above all things whether this swearer was a rich or a poor man, and whether he had children. Being told that nothing was to be got out of him, he ordered that, instead of being fined 5 pounds or 30 florins, he should receive 50 lashes upon his posterior. But as the informer was entitled to one-half of the fine, the Justice asked him if he was willing to forego his half of the poor man's penalty. He answered in the negative, when the Justice bid him have patience, assuring him that he would duly receive his half. He then ordered that 25 good lashes should be administered to the defendant for his profanity. This being done, 25 lashes, well laid on, were administered to the greedy informer, who was not a little surprised at this turn of things. This malignant man vowed, however, that he would never in his life inform again against any one.

In the province of Pennsylvania, and especially in the city of Philadelphia, the Sabbath-breakers who buy and sell on Sunday, when there is no necessity for doing so, are fined 5 pounds or 30 florins for each offence; even a baker who bakes bread and sells it on Sundays or holidays is fined 30 florins. A shopkeeper selling goods on Sunday has still less claim to indulgence. Grinding flour is prohibited

ited under the same penalty. A waggoner or teamster, who drives without necessity into the field or country, has to pay the same fine, because this is considered as his every-day occupation, like that of any other profession. Nevertheless, there is a great confusion on account of the many religious denominations and sects; for especially in the rural districts it is very ill kept. The holidays and apostle-days are not observed at all. As the inhabitants live scattered and often very far from their churches, it happens that many a man keeps divine service with his family in his own house, while many others plough, reap, thresh, hew or split wood and the like, and thus Sunday is disregarded by many. For want of an annual almanac many do not even know when it is Sunday, and thus the young grow up without the necessary divine knowledge, like the aborigines or savages.

In Pennsylvania and the other English colonies there are innumerable negroes, or blacks, who have to serve all their lives as slaves. From 200 to 350 florins are paid for a strong and industrious half-grown negro. Many are given in marriage by their masters in order to raise young blackamoors by them, who are sold in their turn. These blacks are likewise married in the English fashion.

According

According to their color the inhabitants of Pennsylvania may be divided into 4 classes. There are, 1. WHITES, *i. e.* Europeans who have immigrated, and natives begotten by European fathers and mothers; 2. NEGROES, *i. e.* blacks brought over as slaves from Africa; 3. MULATERS or MALATERS [mulattoes], *i. e.* such as are begotten by a white father and a black mother, or by a black father and a white mother; these are neither white nor black, but yellowish; 4. DARK-BROWN, these are the savages or Indians, the old inhabitants of the country.

As to the number of people in Pennsylvania, it must be confessed that the female sex in this new country is very fruitful; for people marry young in this land, and many immigrants arrive every year. In Philadelphia or in the country, when one comes into a house, one finds it usually full of children, and the city of Philadelphia is fairly swarming with them. And if one meets a woman, she is either with child, or she carries a child in her arms, or leads one by the hand. Many children are born every year.* Those that are born and brought up in this country grow very fast; they are full-grown at the age of 15, rarely later than 17 or 18 years

---

* Pennsylvania is said to have 200,000 inhabitants.

but

but they seldom grow old. They resemble herein the trees of their forests. Europeans who emigrate to the country grow much older than those that are born in it. I, at least, have seen few of the latter that were 60 or 70 years old; on the other hand I met people who came to the country as children 75 years ago, with the first immigrants. These told me how it looked in the country at that time, and how much misery they had sometimes to endure. That these beginners in a new and wild country fared very hard, may be readily believed; for this small flock was constantly in great fear on account of the many Indians or savages who swarmed around them at that time; they lacked all sorts of tools, and were compelled to hoe the seed into the soil because they had neither horses nor cattle; besides they were at that time and long afterward without flour-mills, and had to crush the grain between flat stones, so that it was a very difficult task to bake bread. And more than all this, no salt was to be had for a long time. They had wood, and did not lack meat because they shot all sorts of game, though they were often in great want of gun-powder. For a long time several persons had to keep one horse in common until more horses and cattle were brought from other countries. Not to mention the multitude of large

large and small wild beasts, snakes and vermin of every kind, so that they constantly lived in great fear and anxiety; therefore they were obliged to keep large fires burning around their huts by day and by night, to keep the bears, panthers and wolves away. But now bears and panthers are rarely seen in Pennsylvania. A few years ago a large bear came by night into Captain Von Diemer's orchard, and climbed upon the fruit-trees, shaking down apples, just as if a man had been on the trees, so that the dogs began to bark. But the bear did not mind that, and continued shaking. At length the servants notified the master of the house, who went out immediately with two rifles, his servants and dogs, and when he had approached the apple-shaker near enough in the moonlight, he saluted him with a bullet; whereupon the wounded bear growled terribly and tumbled down from the tree topsy-turvy. But as he was about to run away he received a second bullet, and after he had made a somersault and received a third shot, he remained lying on the ground, when the large dogs fell upon him and killed him. This incident filled many neighbors with great joy.

Old people of eighty years and more told me much of their former sad condition; that for a long time there had been a great lack of God-fearing preachers, and the sacraments, baptism and holy communion; and when a preacher occasionally came to a place, many a one was obliged to make a journey of 10, 20, and even 30 hours to hear him; while now most people would not make an hour's trip to hear him, but would even despise him. The many sects lead people astray, and make them heterodox, especially many of our young German folks who are easy to seduce, because they have often many years to serve with them, so that they even forget their mother-tongue. Even many adults and old people have changed their faith, merely for the sake of their sustenance. I could quote many instances, but as this would lead me too far, I shall content myself with relating a single case. I was well acquainted with an old German neighbor, who had been a Lutheran, but had re-baptized himself in a running water; some time afterwards he circumcised himself and believed only in the Old Testament; finally, however, shortly before his death, he baptized himself again by sprinkling water upon his head.

 I cannot pass over another example of the godless life of some people in this free country. Two very rich planters living in Oley township, who were very well known to me, one by the name of Arnold Hufnagel, the other named Conrad

Conrad Reif, both arch-enemies and scoffers of the preachers and the divine word, often met to ridicule and scoff at the ministers and all the church people, and to deny heaven and future salvation, as well as eternal damnation in hell. In 1753 these two scoffers met again one day, according to their evil custom, and began to speak of heaven and hell, said Arnold Hufnagel to Conrad Reif: "How much will you give me for my place in heaven, brother?" Said the other: "I will give you just as much as you will give me for my place in hell." Said Hufnagel again: "If you will give me so and so many sheep for my place in heaven, you shall have it." Replied Reif: "I will give them to you if you will give me so and so many sheep for my place in hell." Thus the two scoffers agreed on their bargain, joking blasphemously about heaven and hell. On the following day as Hufnagel, who had been ready to part with his place in heaven on such cheap terms, was about to descend to his cellar, which had always been his heaven, he suddenly dropped down dead; while Reif was attacked in his field by a flight of so-called golden eagles, which would surely have killed him if he had not cried piteously for help, when some neighbors came to his assistance. From that day he would not trust himself out of his house; he was taken with

with a wasting disease and died in his sins, unrepentant and unshriven. These two examples had the visible effect of arousing the consciousness of other scoffers. For God will not permit Himself to be scoffed.

On the first and second days of the month of May there is general merry-making in Pennsylvania, in which the unmarried persons of both sexes chiefly take part. All amuse themselves with playing, dancing, shooting, hunting, and the like. Such unmarried persons as are born in the country adorn their heads with a piece of the fur of some wild animal, together with any painted animal they may choose. With these the young men walk about the city, crying, "Hurrah! Hurrah!" But no one may put such a token in his hat except those born in the country, and these are called Indians.

In Pennsylvania the following custom prevails among all people, high and low, in the city and in the country. When any one enters a house, or meets another, he first presses the hand of the father and mother of the family; then he salutes in the same manner with his hand all other persons, as many as there may be, and it happens sometimes that he will find a whole room full. Such salutation and handshaking is customary with strangers as well as among the most intimate friends, and the mode

mode of addressing each other is among the English as well as the Germans: "How are you, good friend?" And the answer is: "So middling." This pleasant custom springs in part from the many English Quakers in Philadelphia, and in part from the Indians themselves, who were the first among whom this custom prevailed. To speak the truth, one seldom hears or sees a quarrel among them. Even strangers trust each other more than acquaintances in Europe. People are far more sincere and generous than in Germany; therefore our Americans live more quietly and peacefully together than the Europeans; and all this is the result of the liberty which they enjoy and which makes them all equal.

There are in this country a great many very beautiful pearl-colored squirrels which are as large again as ours. They are shot daily for food, because their flesh is very delicious; they are almost as long as a half-grown hare, but not so thick. Hares, snipe, pheasants, wild ducks, wild pigeons, wild turkeys can be shot in great numbers every day; fish and fowl, too, are everywhere to be had in plenty. And here I remember another kind of squirrel, viz., the flying squirrel,[*] which is exceedingly

---

[*] For a description of this flying squirrel see the German translation of M. De Diereville's Journey to Acadia, p. 239.
pretty;

pretty; but this species is very small, about the size of a rat, though not so thick; you can cover it up with your hand. It can fly the distance of a rifle-shot; its fur is like fine velvet, its color like that of the large squirrel; a good price is paid for its skin. I took such a flying squirrel with me to exhibit in Germany as a rare and marvelous little animal; but in the sixth week at sea it was quite unexpectedly bitten to death by a very large parrot. This parrot had a bright yellow belly and sky-blue wings; it was larger than an ordinary rooster, and could speak much English. There were two other species on board the ship; one was of the size of a pigeon, grass-green and could speak Spanish; the third species was a pair, a he and a she, not much larger than quail, grass-green, with red heads, and they could talk much English. There are many kinds of these strange and beautiful birds in Pennsylvania.

The cultivation of music is rather rare as yet. In the capital city, Philadelphia, no music is made either in the English or in the German churches. Some Englishmen give occasional concerts in private houses with a spinet or harpsichord. I came to the country with the first organ, which now stands in a High German Lutheran church in the city of Philadelphia, and

and which was built in Heilbronn. After this work had been set up and tuned it was consecrated with great rejoicing, and delivered to the Christian St. Michael's Church for the praise and service of God. At this great and joyous festival there appeared 15 Lutheran ministers with the entire vestries of all the Evangelical churches. The crowd of hearers was indescribably large; many people came from a great distance, 10, 20, 30, 40, and even 50 hours' journey, to see and hear this organ. The number of hearers, who stood inside and outside the church, both German and English, were estimated at several thousands. On the 2nd day of this solemn festival of rejoicing a conference was held by all the assembled Lutheran ministers and vestries, and on that occasion I was appointed school-master and organist. As I became more and more known in Pennsylvania, and the people learned that I had brought fine and good instruments with me, many English and German families came 10, 20 and 30 hours' journey to hear them and to see the organ, and they were greatly surprised, because they had never in all their lives seen or heard an organ or any of these instruments.

At the present time there are 6 organs in Pennsylvania—the 1st is in Philadelphia, the 2nd in Germantown, the 3rd in Providence, the 4th in in New Hanover, the 5th in Dulpenhacken (Tulpehocken), and the 6th in Lancaster, all of which came to the country during the 4 years of my sojourn there.

Throughout Pennsylvania men and women dress according to the English fashion. Women wear no hoops, but all that they wear is very fine, neat and costly. The jackets and skirts are cut and sewed in one piece; in front they can be parted. Beneath these they wear handsomely sewed petticoats trimmed with ribbon, but the outer skirts must reach down to the shoes, and are made of cotton, chintz, or other rich and handsome stuffs. All wear daily fine white aprons, on their shoes usually large silver buckles, round their throats fine strings of beads, in their ears costly drops with fine stones, and on their heads fine white hoods embroidered with flowers and trimmed with lace and streamers. Their gloves are made of velvet, silk and the like, usually trimmed with silver or gold lace and beautifully embroidered. Their neckerchiefs are either of velvet or of pure silk, and likewise tastefully embroidered. When they walk or ride they wear blue or scarlet cloaks which only reach down to the waist. On their heads they wear black or beautifully-colored bannerts (bonnets) of taffeta instead of straw hats. These bannerts are of a peculiar structure

structure and serve instead of parasols, but are much prettier. If our women could see such bannerts, they would surely wish to have them likewise.

When they ride on horseback they have costly whips which are elegantly made of fine wire, whalebone and the like. The handles are usually made of red velvet, plush, or tortoise-shell, mother-of-pearl, ivory, some even of solid silver, according to the price that the wearer is willing to pay. Such whips the women take with them when they ride into the country, to the city, or to church; they keep them in their hands even in church. Many a woman is a match in riding for the best horseman. An English servant-woman, especially in Philadelphia, is as elegantly dressed as an aristocratic lady in Germany.

All English ladies are very beautiful; they wear their hair usually cut short or frizzed.

The apparel of the men, especially Englishmen, is very costly, among the farmers as well as among persons of rank; they all wear garments of fine English cloth or other materials, also fine shirts. Every one wears a wig, the peasant as well as the gentleman. In Philadelphia they wear very large and very fine beaver hats, which is no wonder, seeing that this is the home of the beaver. But in summer, on account of the great heat, every one, especially

ially in the country, wears the rim of the hat turned down.

For the same reason thin, light coats or jackets are worn which are neatly made of fine linen or dimity. Every one wears long trousers reaching down to the shoes; these trousers are very wide and made of stiff linen or buckram. All men have their hair cut short in summer time, and they wear only a cap of fine white linen, and over it a hat with the rim not turned up. On entering a house they only doff the hat, but not the cap; and if any one travels only an hour's journey into the country, he wears his long coat, and a pair of boots that are half turned down and reach only to the middle of the calves. This costume is necessary in this country on account of the sudden changes of temperature.

The price of farms in Pennsylvania, especially round Philadelphia, is already quite high; from 30 to 50 florins are paid for an acre, only a day's journey from the city, although the ground is still uncleared forest land. If a place is desired for a homestead, which is already in a habitable and cultivated condition, containing a dwelling-house, barns and good stables, together with meadows, orchards, tilled fields and sufficient woodland, twice as much is asked for it as for uncultivated land, the price being about one hundred

hundred florins per acre. Rich Englishmen have already bought up from the Indians all the remote land far and near, where all is as yet wild and wooded, in order to sell it again to the Europeans who are coming to the country. Our German people who emigrate there do not get land enough for nothing upon which to build a cottage. The price of land is increasing from year to year, especially because the English see that so many people, anxious to own farms or plantations, are coming to the country every year.

In South Carolina, which is 200-250 hours distant from Pennsylvania, an acre of land, which is, however, all forest, may be had for 18 or 20 kreuzers. There one has to go 1, 2, 3 and more hours to reach his nearest neighbor, and to travel 2, 3, 4, and even 8 days to reach a town or a church. Carolina is much warmer than Pennsylvania, for it produces rice in abundance, much cotton and olive oil. On the trees grow nuts as thick as a fist, and when they fall in autumn and are opened they contain a firm ball, which must be forcibly drawn asunder and combed; afterward the wool is washed and bleached till it is as white as snow. Every one there wears cotton garments.

In Pennsylvania all houses are built solidly of free-stone; and when they stand alone, they are generally

generally provided on every side with large English plate-glass windows. Stoves are rarely seen in the rooms; in their stead all houses have French chimneys; the people sit in front of them, drink their good English beer, or smoke a pipe of tobacco. When these chimneys are well built, no smoke escapes into the rooms.

All houses have on both sides two benches, set up about four feet straight out and in front of the house-doors, and roofed like a garden pavilion, the roof resting on two columns. Such outside benches are found in front of all houses, not only in the country, but in the whole city of Philadelphia. Everybody is sitting on them or promenading in front of them in the evening, when the weather is fine. The streets and houses of this city being so straight, one can look half an hour's journey straight ahead. As has been mentioned in the beginning, there are seven main churches in the city, but only one has a steeple attached to it; this, however, is very high and fine. In this whole city there are no more than two small bells, and when they are rung together, divine service begins in all churches. During the last year of my sojourn there the city councils and the church vestries made arrangements to have three bells of various sizes brought over from London in Old

Old England. No church in the country has a steeple, or is provided with a bell or clock; and the people hear all the year round no ringing or striking the hours, which seems very dull to the newcomers, especially in the nighttime, until they are used to it. But almost every one, farmers as well as private persons, makes use of silver watches; they are very generally worn by the English ladies.

In 1754 some French deserters, according to their statements, met with a strange fatality. Two of them came to Philadelphia where they related the following adventure: Seven of their number had deserted from their regiment which had stood at that time beyond the great river Ohio, intending to escape to Carolina. In the wilderness they had gone astray, had wandered over hill and dale, without meeting with any one except occasionally with some savages; thus they had strayed about for 4 weeks. After they had lost said savages out of sight, and after they had eaten up their provisions, they had subsisted for some time on venison, as long as their powder held out; after that was gone, they came across some large rattlesnakes from which they ran away at first in horror; but being pressed hard by hunger, they remembered that the savages were in the habit of eating these reptiles; so they killed some

some of them and ate their flesh, which was by no means hurtful and poisonous, after they had roasted it on the fire. At length, when they had eaten up this loathsome food, and not knowing whither to turn, after they had marched long by day and by night through forests and swamps, and crossed large and small rivers, they became so weak and feeble that they were unable to continue their wandering, and made up their minds that they were doomed to perish by hunger; when the idea struck them to cast lots which of them was to die first; him they would kill and consume his flesh. Their corporal had given this advice, to which they had all assented. The first lot fell upon the corporal himself, who was greatly startled, but said: I would starve to death anyhow, and all of you will not fare better. They bound him immediately, killed and roasted him, and began to eat his flesh, which lasted them a while. In the meantime they continued their march. But soon they were again pressed hard by hunger, and again they cast lots; and thus they went on until two only of the seven were left alive when they met with people; and at length they reached Philadelphia. This long and fatal journey lasted from the beginning of May to the end of June.

There is a current saying to the effect that
Pennsylvania

Pennsylvania is the paradise of women, the purgatory of men, and the hell of horses.

A. D. 1753, Sept. 21st, the new calendar was introduced in Pennsylvania and in all English colonies of America. Accordingly a jump was made from the 11th to the 21st of September. This change met with much opposition from the people as well as the High Church of England and the sects. To some it has been a great grievance that a Sunday was thus left out and lost with its gospel.*

Regarding the climate of Pennsylvania, it must be observed that the summer and winter seasons, as to night and day, differ about 3 hours from those of Europe, the days and nights being shorter or longer than with us. In summer, when the days are longest, about St. John's day, the day does not begin until 4:30 a. m., while at 8 p. m. it is entirely night; again, in winter, when the days are shortest, they are longer here and the nights shorter than in Europe, for at 5:30 a. m. it is fully daylight, while night does not set in until 6 p. m. It is also noteworthy that when the sun has set in America, it is completely dark in one-half of a quarter of an hour, while with us daylight lin-

---

* A strange grievance which would be felt in most years, as the gospels of the 25th, 26th and 27th Sundays after Trinity are often lost in this way.

gers

gers more than half an hour. Observe also this difference, that when the sun has risen in Europe, night still continues for three hours in these American lands; on the other hand, when the sun has set in Europe, it continues to shine for three hours in America. Pennsylvania must, therefore, be very remote from us. I often heard from captains and seamen that according to their calculation the distance across the open sea alone, from land to land, is 3,600 English miles, or 1,200 German hours. As to the depth of the ocean they told me that, at a distance of about 100 miles from the land, the bottom of the sea could no longer be fathomed, though they sunk the sounding-lead with a rope of 50,000 fathoms' length into the sea; which had often been done.

Three great roads have been laid out in the province of Pennsylvania, all of which lead from Philadelphia into the interior of the country as far as it is inhabited. The first road runs from Philadelphia to the right hand by the Delaware to New Frankfurt [Frankford]; the second or middle road runs through Germantown, Rittingston (Reading) and Dulppenhacken (Tulpehocken), extending across the Blue Mountains; the third road runs to the left hand toward Lancaster and Bethlehem, where there is a monastery and nunnery of Dunkers, inhabited by brethren

ren and sisters. The men do not shave their beards; many a one among them has a beard half an ell long. They wear cowls like the Capuchin monks, in winter of the same cloth and color, but in summer of fine white linen. The sisters dress in the same manner. These people are not baptized, which is done by immersion in deep water, until they are fullgrown and can give an account of their faith. Instead of Sunday they keep the preceding Saturday. Their convent-sisters aforesaid frequently bring forth living fruits in patience.

In conclusion I will relate how, on my way home, when the sea was calm and there was no wind, I saw fish without number and of various kinds and sizes. Among these are especially to be noted the large *schorks* (sharks) or man-eaters, of which often whole hosts were floating on the surface of the sea. They are formed like a hog, but as large as an ox, and they blow up the water to a man's height. Many of these fish came so near to the ship that they might have been hit with a stone. They cause, sometimes, a tremendous roar, which always portends a great storm.

In 1750, while I was on my way to America, a large shark was caught and taken on board another ship by means of a hook, to which a piece of meat had been attached; and when they

they opened the monster, they found in its bowels a whole man who still had on his shoes with silver buckles; from which fact it was surmised that this man could not have died a natural death, in which case he would not have been sunk into the water with his shoes and buckles on, but that he must have fallen overboard from carelessness, perhaps during a gale.*

In calm weather I frequently saw at sea many flying fish, which flew so long as they were wet. The largest are about half a foot long, and they have long fins that look like wings. They are much pursued and eaten by other fish. The fish which we caught were always fresh and welcome food for us at sea; they were of diverse beautiful colors, some sky-blue with yellow stars, some gold color with red stars, and others white with blue stars. These fish were usually 4, 5, and even 6 feet long.

On our way home across the sea we passed through two terrific and dangerous gales. The first gale came on a Sunday morning, soon after the beginning of our voyage. During the

---

* This seems to be no other fish than the *Canis carcharias*, called by the Dutch *Hayfisch*, and for which almost every nation has a different name. *Schork* [shark] appears to be its English appellation. [The Dutch name of the shark is *haai*, the German *hai* or *haifisch*.—THE TRANSLATOR.]

storm the sailors had to furl up the sails; but the wind blew so violently into one of the sails that 12 men were unable to manage it, the second mate was obliged to ascend the mainmast. But even this aid was not sufficient. At length the gale tore the sail out of the hands of the sailors and knocked the mate down, so that he fell dead upon the deck of the ship. The storm lasted more than twenty-four hours; the sea went so high that the waves rolled like high mountains over each other, and fell roaring into the ship, so that the man at the helm and the two men that stood at the pump had to be tied fast, lest they should be washed overboard by the waves. At that time we gave ourselves up as lost together with the ship.

In the seventh week, Sept. 22nd, we had another gale which was so terrific that the sailors were unable to furl up all the sails. The wind blew so violently that it tore one of the largest sails into shreds, though it had been tied fast with immensely thick ropes. The waves of the sea were indescribably formidable, so that the ship now rode on their crests, and was now tossed down into an abyss, was now hurled upon one side, and now upon the other. The billows rolled constantly over the ship, so that every one thought that it would go down with all on board. This gale and terrible anxiety lasted
from

from four o'clock in the evening until toward three o'clock of the second night, when the wind subsided, but the sea was that whole day still so wild and high, and the ship rocked and rolled so violently that it was impossible to cook a meal or to take any comfort. The poultry on board the ship was mostly found dead, the pigs and sheep were sick, and the crew of the ship themselves were more dead than alive.

At length the end of our return voyage approached. On the last day of the eighth week the captain called his mates and ordered them to furl up all the sails, and when this was done, to throw out the sounding-lead to see if it reached the bottom. This being done, the sounding-lead touched bottom at a depth of 72 fathoms, a circumstance which filled us passengers with great joy, because we could hope now to soon see land. This hope did not deceive us, for on the fourth day of the ninth week we came near the headland of Old England. This headland looks white as snow, and the land is therefore called Albion. But as we came nearer the land, and had turned on our right a large corner of France, we struck a sandbank, so that the ship threatened to sink. But fortunately the tide had just set in, and we had a good strong wind which buoyed the ship up and made an end to our tribulation, God be praised.
Thus,

Thus, after nine weeks, on the 10th of October, A. D. 1754, after many perils and hardships, we entered the Thames at London and landed safely on the same day on which, four years before, I had trod the soil of America. We all thanked God from the bottom of our hearts; I kissed the ground with joy, and took well to heart the 107th Psalm, which describes the anguish of the seafarers so faithfully:

> To the Triune GOD, for this great mercy and preservation be praise and thanksgiving rendered now and evermore.

www.ingramcontent.com/pod-product-compliance
Lightning Source LLC
Chambersburg PA
CBHW020111170426
43199CB00009B/492